THE BARCLAY HOTEL

THE BARCLAY HOTEL

New York's Elegant Hideaway for the Rich and Famous

CINDY GUELI AND WARD MOREHOUSE III

Published by BearManor Media
New York, New York
2013

Copyright © 2013 by Cindy Gueli and Ward Morehouse III.
All Rights Reserved.

No part of this book may be reproduced in any form or by any means, electronic, mechanical, digital, photocopying or recording, except for the inclusion in a review, without permission in writing from the publisher.

Library of Congress Cataloging-in-Publication Data

Gueli, Cynthia.
  The Barclay Hotel : New York's elegant hideaway for the rich and famous / by Cindy Gueli and Ward Morehouse III.
    pages cm
  Includes bibliographical references and index.
  ISBN 978-1-59393-264-0 (alkaline paper)
  1. Barclay Hotel (New York, N.Y.)--History. 2. New York (N.Y.)--Social life and customs--20th century. 3. New York (N.Y.)--Biography. 4. Rich people--New York (State)--New York--Biography. 5. Celebrities--New York (State)--New York--Biography. I. Morehouse, Ward. II. Title.
  TX941.B365G83 2013
  647.9409747'1--dc23
                                                          2013023744

Published in the USA by:
BearManor Media
PO Box 1129
Duncan, Oklahoma 73534-1129
www.bearmanormedia.com

Printed in the United States of America
Cover and book design by Bob Antler, Antler Designworks

Table of Contents

Introduction...7

CHAPTER 1:
Setting the Stage for The Barclay...11

CHAPTER 2:
All That Roaring, Soaring Jazz:
New York in the Twenties...21

CHAPTER 3:
Pauline Sabin: Unlikely Crusader...29

CHAPTER 4:
Mike Vanderbilt:
"Wealth and Wit and Sportsmanship"...35

SIDEBAR:
NYC-3 Rolls by Ward Morehouse III...40

CHAPTER 5:
Caswell-Massey: Chemists to the Stars...43

CHAPTER 6:
"The Hostess with the Mostest!"...47

CHAPTER 7:
The Barclay Through World War II...57

CHAPTER 8:
Papa Hemingway and the Forties...63

CHAPTER 9:
The Iceman Cometh to The Barclay...67

CHAPTER 10:
Welcome to the Club...73

CHAPTER 11:
The Barclay Through the 1970s...79

CHAPTER 12:
Martin Luther King, Jr.:
A Conversation for Change...85

CHAPTER 13:
Glitterati...89

CHAPTER 14:
Becoming InterContinental...93

CHAPTER 15:
Looking Forward...99

Selected Bibliography...103

Introduction

In contrast to the boisterous parties one might expect from a decade known as the Roaring Twenties, The Barclay's Board of Directors officially opened the hotel on November 4, 1926 with a sedate but lavish eight-course, French-themed dinner. Chefs prepared a culinary extravaganza starting with fresh Beluga caviar and finishing with *le coup glacée Barclay avec les friandises* (a frozen dessert decorated with colorful bite-sized candies adapted and named expressly for the occasion). After the meal, residents and invited guests mingled on the dance floor to the orchestra's smooth renditions of hit songs "Dinah" and "Bye, Bye, Blackbird." Elegantly dressed couples circled in waltzes and fox-trots, a far cry from the iconic period image of short-skirted flappers turning out a racy Charleston. The event epitomized the style and theme of the new hotel—gracious, reserved, and exclusive.

Newspapers covered the event as a gathering of the who's who on the New York social registry. Luminaries included inaugural tenants Edward Dimon Bird, a director of the world famous jeweler Tiffany & Co.; Frederic de Zaldo, owner of substantial tobacco and sugar plantations in his native Cuba; and Finley P. Dunne, creator of the sensationally popular satirical character "Mr. Dooley," and his wife Margaret Abbott, the first American woman to win an Olympic gold medal. These and the other trendsetters retired to their lavishly decorated apartments after listening to welcoming remarks by Eliot Cross, Board Chairman and co-owner of Cross & Cross, the architectural firm that designed the hotel.

Another board member and opening night guest was William Seward Webb, Jr. He traced his roots back to Cornelius "Commodore" Vanderbilt, founder of the family dynasty. The larger-than-life industrialist earned his nautical nickname from the ferry service he started as a teenager. He made one fortune by building that single boat into a vast shipping empire and another by investing those earnings in railroads. When the Commodore died in 1877, his estate was worth about $26 billion in today's currency. By the 1920s, Vanderbilt's New York-based company, whose holdings included Grand Central Terminal and much of its surrounding land, was still mostly owned, if not necessarily operated, by his great-grandchildren. The family's wealth and prestige remained a powerful presence in New York society.

Many people involved with the development of The Barclay, as well as several early residents, were connected to the hotel through the Vanderbilts. New York was the largest city in the country but high society was still a small, insular network.

Most of the residents in those first few decades used the hotel as a pied-à-terre as they traveled the country to coincide with the social seasons. The Barclay regularly forwarded residents' mail to Palm Beach, Newport, the Adirondacks, and other fashionable resorts. This was one of the reasons apartment hotels became popular in the 1920s (and the same reasons they are making a comeback today)—convenience and service without the long-term responsibility or commitment. An early advertisement for The Barclay boasts that becoming a resident "relieves you of the daily details of living."

But also like contemporary residential hotels, comfort and amenities came at a steep price. The Barclay was strictly outfitted for upscale living. As the clientele broadened over the years from mostly blue-blooded socialites to include writers, celebrities, politicians, diplomats, and business people, the number of long-term residents decreased and the hotel phased out yearly leases. The function if not the essence of The Barclay evolved over time.

In the history of New York hotels, The Barclay often slips under

Introduction 9

the radar. The very elements that made it a perfect hideaway for the rich and famous kept it out of the glare of the media spotlight. But its story can give us a glimpse into the people and lifestyles that defined each generation; the local, national and international events that impacted and changed New York City; and what it takes to survive almost ninety years in one of the most thrilling, unpredictable, and influential cities in the world.

This is the story of The Barclay and some of the incredible people who called it home.

The grand concept for Terminal City began in 1902 with William J. Wilgus, an engineer for the New York Central Railroad. The Biltmore Hotel to the left of the train station hosted the Grand Central Art Galleries for over twenty years showcasing work by renowned artists such as John Singer Sargent and Edmund Greacen in its six exhibition rooms.

Setting the Stage for The Barclay

In 1925 The Barclay Park Corporation leased a plot of land on the west side of Lexington Avenue at 48th Street from the New York Central Railroad in order to built an exclusive fourteen-story residential hotel. The syndicate of investors included friends and business partners William Seward Webb, Jr. and Eliot Cross. Both men came from socially prominent families whose network of connections helped fund and occupy their ventures in real estate.

Webb was a great-grandson of Cornelius "Commodore" Vanderbilt, patriarch of the family dynasty. Webb's pedigreed upbringing included graduating from the prestigious Groton School and Yale University. He worked as a clerk for banking magnate J. P. Morgan and as a stockbroker before serving in World War I. His real estate career began in earnest after the war but his friendship with Eliot Cross started much earlier. They moved in the same elite circles.

Cross opened the architectural firm Cross & Cross with his brother John in 1907. John Walter Cross held degrees from Groton, Yale, and École des Beaux-Arts in Paris (the prestigious school known for training many architects responsible for reconstructing Paris into a city of grand boulevards and monumental public buildings) and served as the creative force behind the company. Eliot, who graduated from Groton and Harvard University, managed the business aspects of the firm. Eliot also chaired The Barclay Park Corporation, one of many real estate projects he headed up throughout the city.

Cross & Cross already had a strong reputation for the elegant

"In town it is no longer quite in taste to build marble palaces, however much money one may have," noted Arthur Pound, a New York writer and cultural observer in the 1920s. *"Instead, one lives in a hotel."*

yet distinctive designs coveted by the city's upper crust. They created plans for residential properties—including Webb's Long Island estate in 1916—but earned lasting notoriety for prodigious and influential commercial work around Manhattan like the Tiffany & Co. flagship store on Fifth Avenue at 56th Street and the fifty-story terra-cotta brick General Electric Building on Lexington Avenue and 51st Street. The company's design for The Barclay more closely resembles the spare style familiar to their smaller-scale residential and apartment buildings rather than their later Art Deco work on tall office structures.

Setting the Stage for The Barclay 13

Eliot Cross and William Seward Webb, Jr. brought their financial and real estate talents together on many business and construction ventures in New York, not all of which Cross & Cross designed. One of Webb and Cross's early projects as founding partners (along with Robert Knapp) in the company Webb & Knapp, Inc. was redeveloping a small residential area of brownstones bordering the East River called Sutton Place. They declared that the neighborhood would be a new hub for elite New Yorkers and accordingly sold homes to cultural leaders like philanthropist and women's rights advocate Anne Morgan, the daughter of J. P. Morgan, and pioneering interior designer Elsie de Wolfe. Fifty years later Morgan's home was donated to the United Nations and now serves as the Secretary General's official residence. Webb and Cross bought several properties in the enclave for themselves and family members but saved 1 Sutton Place, a newly built four-story brownstone, for Anne Vanderbilt who wanted to leave behind her massive, chateau-style mansion and the encroaching commercial development on Fifth Avenue.

Anne was the widow of William Kissam Vanderbilt, head of the family's business interests for his generation. He was also William Seward Webb, Jr.'s uncle. Webb's mother (Eliza Osgood Vanderbilt) and William Kissam were brother and sister. Webb's father was also a real estate developer and a director of the New York Central Railroad. It was through these family contacts that Webb was able to acquire the air rights over 111 48th Street for The Barclay Park Corporation's plan to build a hotel.

This parcel of land was created when the rail lines leading into the newly rebuilt Grand Central Terminal were covered over in 1913. The Terminal, the rail lines, and most of the surrounding land were part of the Vanderbilt holdings. The modern terminal replaced a succession of previous depots that existed on the site since 1871. A regulatory change from steam-powered to electric trains allowed for miles of open tracks in the city to be buried underground. The New York State Realty and Terminal Company, a division of the New York Central Railroad, leased the air rights over these reclaimed

THE BARCLAY HOTEL

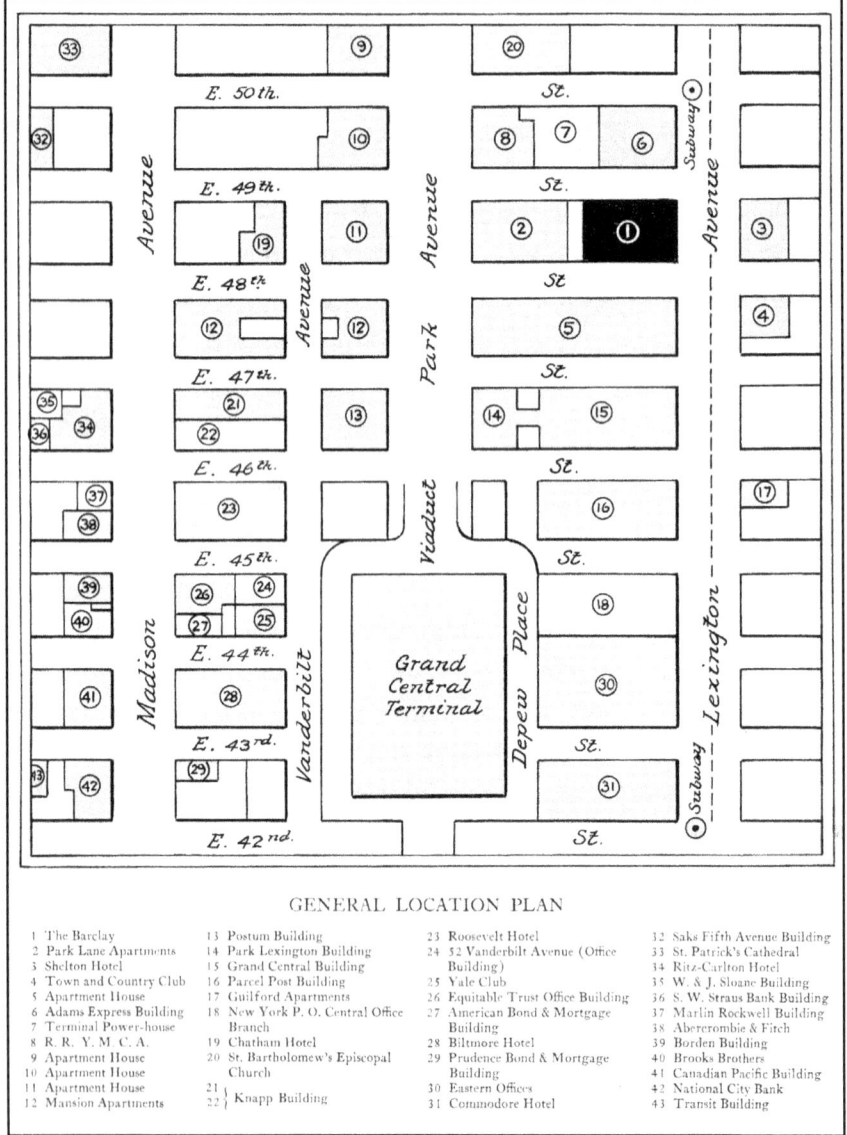

GENERAL LOCATION PLAN

1. The Barclay
2. Park Lane Apartments
3. Shelton Hotel
4. Town and Country Club
5. Apartment House
6. Adams Express Building
7. Terminal Power-house
8. R. R. Y. M. C. A.
9. Apartment House
10. Apartment House
11. Apartment House
12. Mansion Apartments
13. Postum Building
14. Park Lexington Building
15. Grand Central Building
16. Parcel Post Building
17. Guilford Apartments
18. New York P. O. Central Office Branch
19. Chatham Hotel
20. St. Bartholomew's Episcopal Church
21. } Knapp Building
22.
23. Roosevelt Hotel
24. 52 Vanderbilt Avenue (Office Building)
25. Yale Club
26. Equitable Trust Office Building
27. American Bond & Mortgage Building
28. Biltmore Hotel
29. Prudence Bond & Mortgage Building
30. Eastern Offices
31. Commodore Hotel
32. Saks Fifth Avenue Building
33. St. Patrick's Cathedral
34. Ritz-Carlton Hotel
35. W. & J. Sloane Building
36. S. W. Straus Bank Building
37. Marlin Rockwell Building
38. Abercrombie & Fitch
39. Borden Building
40. Brooks Brothers
41. Canadian Pacific Building
42. National City Bank
43. Transit Building

The Barclay is the black square numbered "1." The other railroad hotels are the Roosevelt at 23, Biltmore at 28 and Commodore at 31. Numbers 6, 7, and 8 will become the Waldorf Astoria and Number 2 The Park Lane Hotel.

streets—about 30 blocks on the East Side of Manhattan—in order to create a coordinated hub of commercial, retail, and residential development known as Terminal City. This early twentieth-century building boom transformed the character of Midtown into a village of brick and masonry skyscrapers.

Fashionable, upscale apartments and hotels started rising on the blocks north of Grand Central Terminal. Between 1923 and 1928 over $100 million was invested in the redevelopment of Lexington Avenue between 42nd and 52nd Streets. Land values increased over 300 percent during that same period making it an exclusive and desirable neighborhood.

The Barclay was one of four "railroad hotels" associated with the Terminal City project. Each one literally connected to Grand Central through specially designed underground passages. Theoretically, business travelers could arrive by train into New York City, spend the night at a railroad hotel, go to Wall Street via subway, return to their hotel, and catch a train back home without ever setting foot outdoors.

The 1,000-room Biltmore was the first to open in 1913 covering an entire block at 43rd Street and Madison Avenue. The 29-story luxury hotel stood adjacent to Grand Central Terminal. It was designed by Warren and Wetmore, one of the firms responsible for the Terminal itself. Architect Whitney Warren was yet another connection to the Vanderbilt family. Whitney Warren, one of the architects, was yet another connection to the Vanderbilt family. He was a first cousin to William Kissam Vanderbilt.

Several public spaces in The Biltmore were linked directly to the station and therefore became popular places for people to meet—especially under the solid bronze clock in the hotel lobby and in the long distance arrival room fondly referred to as the "kissing room." Beverly Sills, the famed soprano and former general director of the New York City Opera, reminisced about the hotel's allure to *The New York Times*. "When I was a kid growing up in Coney Island I had a lot of boyfriends in the Bronx and I wanted to meet them

The Hotel Commodore was built next to Grand Central Terminal in 1919. Some of this old masonry facade still exists behind the glass covering installed in the 1970s when it was converted into a Grand Hyatt.

under the clock," she remembered. "My father thought that nice young girls didn't meet boys in hotel lobbies, so I never made it."

F. Scott and Zelda Fitzgerald did make it to The Biltmore. But they caused so much commotion while staying there on their honeymoon that the management asked the couple to leave. The renowned author used the hotel as a setting for "Myra Meets His Family," the first of his stories published in the *Saturday Evening Post*, permanently tying The Biltmore to "Jazz Age" culture. Fitzgerald later coined that very term and helped define the era with *The Great Gatsby*. Thirty years later J. D. Salinger used The Biltmore's lobby as a meeting place for Holden Caulfield's date in his controversial novel *The Catcher in the Rye* securing the hotel's place in literary history.

The 24-story Commodore Hotel at 42nd Street and Lexington Avenue opened in 1919. Contemporary observers proclaimed it had the "most beautiful lobby in the world" in large part due to an elaborate indoor waterfall designed by noted Italian artist John B. Smeraldi. Its main ballroom was big enough for—and indeed once accommodated—a three-ring circus complete with elephants.

The 2,000-room hotel was named for Commodore Vanderbilt whose statue still sits on The Grand Central Driveway which wraps around the mammoth station. This hotel was also designed by Warren and Wetmore and at one point operated by Webb & Knapp, Inc., the company whose partners included both William Seward Webb, Jr. and Eliot Cross. Cross & Cross would also be brought in to design a 1937 renovation and modernization of the hotel.

The Roosevelt on 45th Street and Madison Avenue was the third hotel connected to Grand Central Terminal, opening in 1924. George B. Post & Sons, famous for designing the New York Stock Exchange and Cornelius Vanderbilt II's palatial 130-room mansion on Fifth Avenue and 57th Street, planned the 22-story building in the same Italian Renaissance-style as many other buildings associated with Terminal City. It was the first hotel in the city to make use of setbacks, a provision of New York's first zoning regulation in 1916 that allowed additional building height for every foot it was set

The Roosevelt was one of four "railroad hotels" connected to Grand Central Terminal through underground passageways as part of the grand concept for New York Central Railroad's Terminal City.

back from the street. Setbacks would evolve into the dominant New York architectural style of the era.

The 1,100-room Roosevelt became renowned as the host of Guy Lombardo and his Orchestra, who performed there for over thirty years (before being wooed away by The Waldorf-Astoria). Their live broadcast featuring a midnight rendition of "Auld Lang Syne" became a favorite New Year's Eve tradition for millions of people around the country. The hotel also served as a popular setting for films such as *Wall Street, Maid in Manhattan,* and *The French Connection.*

The Barclay, built in 1926, was the last of the railroad hotels. It was also the furthest north and smallest of the four at fourteen stories and 880 rooms. The sales literature advertised its allure: "The Barclay is essentially a residential hotel. It has neither ball-room, grill-room nor convention hall, but it has that atmosphere and that quality of equipment and service that one associates in one's mind with a great private house." No crowds of reunited travelers, rooftop dining, musical broadcasts, or cavernous ballrooms. It had the greatest number of residential units of the sister hotels. A stay at The Barclay was intended to mimic the quiet retreat of home.

But not the average home. Architecture critic Christopher Gray explained the hotel's style in a 2009 newspaper column: "The expansive 1926 Barclay was designed by Cross & Cross as a hotel version of a Park Avenue apartment house, with beautiful limestone on the ground floor, rich with fossil shells and sea creatures, and a façade as confident and debonair as Gene Kelly on a dance floor." The hotel offered a uniquely different form of elegance than its sister hotels.

The Barclay received one of the best testaments possible to its high-end appeal. Both William Seward Webb, Jr. and Eliot Cross chose to live in the hotel they helped build and design. The men and their families, who each had virtually every option available to them, used The Barclay as their New York City home for many years. They were joined by some of the most influential and well-known people of their era.

The black marble used in The Barclay's entryway remains an elegant reminder of the hotel's storied past. Long-term residents had use of a smaller, private entrance away from the public spaces.

All That Roaring, Soaring Jazz: New York in the Twenties

The Barclay opened in a city awash with new wealth, feverish growth, and seemingly endless possibilities. As the name suggests, the Roaring Twenties was an era marked by prosperity, innovation, social mobility, and cultural change. Modern America was born and New York City was its cradle.

The nation's largest metropolitan area boasted a population of nearly six million residents (compared to nineteen million in 2012). About ten percent of the country's agricultural products, raw materials, and manufactured goods originated from New York, and nearly half of the country's imports and exports moved through its bustling harbor and railroad terminals.

Vigorous economic growth—Gross National Product increased an average of 4.2 percent per year—raised incomes and reduced prices. New York City's unemployment rate remained under seven percent for the entire decade. The average American lived better, longer, and more comfortably than ever before. The advent of modern conveniences like electricity, refrigerators, washing machines, and vacuum cleaners made home life easier and created more leisure time to enjoy it.

Higher standards of living led to a dramatic increase in consumer consumption. Kathleen Morgan Drowne and Patrick Huber write about the development of mass consumer culture in *The 1920s*: "Purchasing new clothes, new furniture, new appliances, new automobiles, new *anything* indicated one's level of prosperity, and the ability to consume represented an important social marker in the 1920s."

Yet, New York was still one of the most expensive cities in the world, and living in style at The Barclay cost more than most people could afford. Opening rates at the hotel ranged from $1,400 to $3,600 per year. This was comparable to a high-end Park Avenue apartment where the yearly rent for two rooms at 48th Street ran $2,450 and seven rooms went for $6,800.

But Americans earned an average salary of $2,010 per year, not nearly enough for a luxurious Midtown East apartment. After spending $0.10 to buy a loaf of bread, $0.39 per pound for a chicken or rib roast, $0.45 for a pound of coffee, and $0.20 for a quart of milk, most New Yorkers could not even consider housing options in Terminal City.

Instead, they shelled out a more reasonable $300-$600 year to rent two or three rooms in older, more densely packed areas of Man-

This 1920s postcard shows the main entrance of The Barclay under the awning and flags on the left and its row of storefronts lining Lexington Avenue on the right.

THE BARCLAY
RENTING SCHEDULE

Room Number	2 Floor	3 Floor	4-5 Floor	6-7 Floor	8-9-10 Floor	11-12-13 Floor	14 Floor
1		1300	1400	1450	1550	1700	1750
2-3		2500	2700	2800	3000	3400	3500
4		1350	1450	1500	1600	1650	1700
5-6-7		3700	4000	4150	4450	5200	5350
8		1500	1600	1650	1750	1800	1850
9-10		2600	2800	2900	3100	3600	3700
11		1500	1600	1650	1750	1750	1800
12-13		2700	2900	3000	3200	3700	3800
14		1450	1550	1600	1700	1750	1800
15-16		2650	2850	2950	3150	3500	3600
17		1300	1400	1550	1550	1600	1650
18-19		2400	2600	2700	2900	3200	3300
20		1450	1550	1600	1700	1750	1800
21		1450	1550	1600	1700	1750	1800
22-23		2700	2900	3000	3200	3500	3600
24		1400	1500	1550	1650	1700	1750
25-26-27		3600	3900	4050	4350	5000	5150
28-29		2400	2600	2700	2900	3200	3300
30-31		2600	2800	2900	3100	3400	3500
32		1300	1400	1450	1550	1650	1700
33-34		2500	2700	2800	3000	3300	3400
35		1300	1400	1450	1550	1650	1700
36		1300	1400	1450	1550	1650	1700
37-38		2600	2800	2900	3100	3500	3600
39		1400	1500	1550	1650	1700	1750
40-41	2400	2600	2800	2900	3100	3600	3700
42	1300	1400	1500	1550	1650	1750	1800
43	1300	1400	1500	1550	1650	1750	1800
44-45	2200	2400	2600	2700	2900	3300	3400
46	1200	1300	1400	1450	1550	1700	1750
47-48	2300	2500	2700	2800	3000	3500	3600
49	1300	1400	1500	1550	1650	1750	1800
50-51	2300	2500	2700	2800	3000	3500	3600
52	1300	1400	1500	1550	1650	1800	1850
53-54	2500	2700	2900	3000	3200	3800	3900
55	1350	1450	1550	1600	1700	1800	1850
56-57-58	3500	3800	4100	4250	4550	5400	5550
59	1400	1500	1600	1650	1750	1800	1850
60-61	2500	2700	2900	3000	3200	3600	3700
62	1300	1400	1500	1550	1650	1800	1850
63-64		2800	3000	3100	3300	3600	3700
65		1450	1550	1600	1700	1750	1800
66-67		2700	2900	3000	3200	3500	3600
68-69		2800	3000	3100	3300	3500	3600

Above prices are for unfurnished rooms and subject to change without notice.

As seen in this 1926 rate chart, The Barclay charged $3,600.00 a year to rent Room 68 on the fourteenth floor. A three-bedroom luxury apartment in the same neighborhood can rent for between $7,000 and $13,950 per month today.

More economical than housekeeping, as comfortable and quiet as your home. Relieves you of the daily details of living. Before making your Winter plans, look through the Barclay. Rates are commensurate with the times, term leases being especially attractive.

The BARCLAY

111 EAST 48th STREET
WARREN T. MONTGOMERY—Managing Director

hattan or neighboring boroughs of Queens, Brooklyn and the Bronx. Luckily, the city's transit system recently expanded and New Yorkers could commute for a nickel on the subway or ride a bus through the Holland Tunnel to Manhattan's first bus depot. These were cheaper alternatives to spending close to $350 for a new car.

Many of these commuters were relatively recent immigrants. The foreign-born population of New York tripled between 1880 and 1920. While quota systems implemented in the 1920s ended the major waves of mass migration, new residents still arrived every day. Attracted by the booming economy, workers from other parts of the U.S. also flooded into New York. These new residents played a crucial part in the city's dynamic social, economic, and cultural life but also sometimes clashed with older, more established residents as was the case in the 1926 East Harlem Riots.

Harlem was also the site of what would become one of the twentieth century's greatest artistic movements. Its vibrant music scene attracted extraordinary talent from around the country and packed music halls like the Cotton Club every night. Jazz icon Duke Ellington debuted there in 1927. Other legends such as Louis Armstrong, Jelly Roll Morton, Bessie Smith, and King Oliver helped create a new soundtrack for the city and the time period, helping give rise to Fitzgerald's nickname, The Jazz Age. When included with the influential and renowned works of literature, art, and political philosophy that originated in this African-American community, the new style of music became part of the cultural explosion known as the Harlem Renaissance.

New York was also headquarters for other forms of popular entertainment. The nascent radio industry opened gleaming studios to broadcast round-the-clock programming from Midtown. Radio Row, "the greatest agglomeration of radio dealers' shops in the world," sold transmitters to clients around the world on the Lower West Side. Sixty percent of American families bought radios between 1923 and 1930.

They also went to the movies. By the end of the 1920s, three-quarters of all New Yorkers saw at least one film every week. People flocked to see silent film stars such as Charlie Chaplin, Mary Pickford, and Greta Garbo, hear the first recorded soundtrack in 1926, and witness the first full-length talking picture in 1927. Films became so popular that fear of their influence over public morals instigated the creation of the Motion Picture Producers and Distributors of America (MPPDA), Hollywood's attempt at self regulation in order to avoid stricter federal controls. The MPPDA offices were located in Manhattan, ostensibly away from the possible corruption of Hollywood.

Glittering with newly installed neon lights, Broadway's Great White Way flourished with groundbreaking, diverse productions that would become classics like *No, No, Nanette, The Emperor Jones, Anna Christie,* and *Show Boat.* In 1927 alone, 264 new plays opened, supported by record-shattering ticket sales. During this same era, Tin Pan Alley, New York's fabled music publishing district, produced close to ninety percent of all commercial songs written in America. Popular composers George Gershwin, Aaron Copeland, and Irving Berlin drove sales of records and sheet music into the millions.

One thing Jazz Age New Yorkers could not do for entertainment was drink. At least, not legally. The Eighteenth Amendment to the U.S. Constitution prohibited the sale and manufacture of alcohol as of January 1, 1920. Intended to combat the perceived evils of drunkenness, the amendment and accompanying laws created new problems instead. Criminal gangs and corrupt politicians—many of the most notorious of them based in New York—saw opportunities to make fortunes by making and selling illegal alcohol. By 1925, New York reportedly had anywhere from 30,000 to 100,000 speakeasies. Although crime rates resulting from the "underground" syndicates became more public, the fourteen years Prohibition was enacted did not necessarily make New York an inherently more dangerous city. From 1900 to 1958, New York

City had lower homicide rates than the U.S. as a whole.

The Roaring Twenties came to a catastropic halt with the stock market crash of 1929. But the cultural transitions that it instigated ushered in the modern era for New York as well as the rest of the country. It was into this whirlwind of economic changes, life-changing technology, artistic explosion, and social upheaval that The Barclay sought to create an oasis of quiet, elegance, and classic charm for those lucky enough to live there.

Pauline Sabin's fight to repeal prohibition gave the movement a respectability owing to her elite social status and political connections. Sabin poses with her sons from her first marriage, Paul and James H. Smith, Jr. in 1922. James carried on the family tradition of public service by eventually becoming Assistant Secretary of the Navy and head of the U.S. Agency for International Development.

Pauline Sabin: Unlikely Crusader

In keeping with its attempt to attract a highly select clientele who wanted a refined, residential atmosphere, The Barclay's interior design resembled an eighteenth-century manor house more than a standard hotel. Much of its original look and style was influenced by Pauline Morton Smith Sabin, chairwoman of the advisory committee on decorations and one of The Barclay's first tenants.

Sabin came from a politically and economically influential family. Her grandfather, Julius Sterling Morton, was governor of Nebraska and later Secretary of Agriculture. One of his legacies was the creation of Arbor Day, which is still celebrated on his birthday every year. Her father, Paul Morton, was a railroad executive and Secretary of the Navy. And her uncle, Joy Morton, founded Morton Salt Company. Sabin grew up with an insider's understanding of politics and a debutante's flair for style and presentation.

After a brief first marriage (the lavish wedding of which was attended by social arbiters like President Theodore Roosevelt, the Astors, and the Carnegies), Sabin married Charles Hamilton Sabin, president of J. P. Morgan's Guaranty Trust Company. She used her position as a wealthy, well-connected New York socialite to launch into party politics. She was an energetic, charismatic woman with strong convictions. Despite her husband's (and father's) affiliation with the Democratic Party, Sabin became the first woman representative to the Republican National Committee and a delegate to both Republican National Conventions in the 1920s. But it was her vehement opposition to Prohibition that gained her national notoriety.

The Metropolitan Museum of Art's "Baltimore Room," taken from a 19th century Maryland townhouse, served as the model for one of The Barclay's original 1926 private dining rooms.

Sabin at first supported the national ban on the sale, manufacture, and transportation of alcohol. But she was appalled at the hypocrisy she witnessed by politicians who voted to outlaw alcohol and then expected drinks at dinner parties. Sabin also came to believe the ban increased instead of decreased alcohol-related violence. At a Republican event held in her honor in 1929, she dramatically resigned from the Party to form the nonpartisan Women's Organization for National Prohibition Reform. The group's only goal was to repeal the Eighteenth Amendment. It was a leading force in accomplishing that objective in 1933.

During this same time period, Sabin arranged to take an apartment at The Barclay. She added her panache and expertise to that of R. T. H. Halsey, creator of the American Wing of the Metropolitan Museum of Art in 1924, to direct the furnishing and decorating of the hotel. Halsey worked on the New York Stock Exchange for almost twenty years before he retired in order to devote his full time to the Museum. He took an academic interest in decorative arts and wrote and lectured extensively on how material items revealed a deeper understanding of American history. He, like Sabin, maintained an exclusive collection of Americana. The two worked together to develop the interior style of The Barclay, employing the decorating department at W. & J. Sloane furniture store and even letting pieces from their private collections be copied for use in the hotel.

Sabin had another connection to the hotel that also influenced its initial design. In 1918 she hired brothers John and Eliot Cross to draw up plans for her 28-room, English-style manor house on Long Island. Critics heralded Cross & Cross's design for Sabin's Bayberry Land, and the house and gardens generated much attention and publicity. As the Cross brothers developed and designed The Barclay just a few years later, Sabin's interest and involvement in the project naturally followed.

The idea of designing the atmosphere of The Barclay after a well-heeled manor house filled with references to American decorative and cultural history made sense under the influence of Sabin, Halsey, and Cross & Cross. It served as a counterpoint to the recent emergence of the Art Deco style as the model for modern, sophisticated décor.

George Washington's Mount Vernon home was cited as inspiration for the layout and simplicity of the lobby and guest room interiors. Motifs celebrating early American colonial history were integrated into the rugs, cornices, window fixtures, and lamps. Wallpaper lining the hallways depicted images copied from a rare British print from 1720 showing New York City in that same year. Faithful reproductions of nineteenth-century Duncan Phyfe furniture were scattered throughout the hotel's lobbies and hallways. The look might seem sparse and possibly kitschy to contemporary

Architectural details in the hotel's lobby reflect the original design pattern based on early American ornamental motifs such as eagles, arrows, and pineapples.

tastes. But the effect was elegant, restrained, and proper during a time when excess and frivolity was becoming more associated with mass culture than Gilded Age wealth.

The second floor of The Barclay offered three private dining rooms for residents who wanted to entertain. One of them was a near-perfect copy of the Baltimore Room at the Metropolitan Museum of Art. The floor plan and furniture duplicated the parlor of a wealthy merchant living in early nineteenth-century Maryland. This gave guests the experience of dining in a townhouse from America's Federal period. Twelve special suites were outfitted with Early American, French Provincial, or Louis XVI furniture duplicated from originals held at the Museum.

The attention to detail could not have been more exact had Sabin, Halsey, and the decoration committee chosen interiors for their own homes. And that's precisely the feeling they wanted to evoke. Sabin planned political campaigns from her rooms, no doubt being reminded by the arrows, stars, liberty caps, and eagles to fight for the freedoms she believed were due to the American people. She made the cover of *Time* magazine in July 1932 for an accompanying article highlighting the "Sabin sisterhood" and their crusade.

By the late 1930s Sabin was widowed, remarried to former Secretary of War Dwight Davis (known in tennis circles for lending his name and money to the Davis Cup), and mostly splitting her time between Washington, D.C. and her Bayberry Land homes. Her interest in architecture and style honed at The Barclay led her to become one of the founding members of the National Trust for Historic Preservation. When she died in 1955, she left behind a legacy to The Barclay, New York, and the nation.

Mike Vanderbilt's immense family wealth allowed him to enjoy a rarefied lifestyle filled with yachts, mansions, international travel, private rail cars, and a two-story rooftop apartment at The Barclay. The avid sailor successfully defended the America's Cup trophy three times in a row during the 1930s.

Mike Vanderbilt:
"Wealth and Wit and Sportsmanship"

Harold Stirling Vanderbilt, known as *Mike* to his friends, brought in his own interior decorators to outfit his seventeen-room duplex apartment on the top floor of The Barclay. The circular staircase of onyx and marble, bedrooms paneled in antique French oak, private rooftop squash court and gymnasium, and portraits of his illustrious ancestors created a distinctive Midtown sanctuary. The furnishings were likely inspired by his upbringing at "Petit Château," the French Renaissance mansion built by his parents William K. and Alva Vanderbilt. (It was also this home on Fifth Avenue that Anne Vanderbilt, William K.'s second wife, sold in order to move into Sutton Place.)

William Seward Webb, Jr., one of the developers and fellow residents of The Barclay, was Mike Vanderbilt's first cousin. They were both great-grandsons of Commodore Vanderbilt. Social connections—through both family and friends—ran rampant through the halls of the first generation of residents at The Barclay.

In 1927 *Town Topics: The Journal of Society*, a magazine published to chronicle New York's high society activities and scandals, proclaimed, "Whether true or not, it has been said that one of the unwritten requisites of being a tenant of The Barclay is to be in the Social Register." The Register was a mark of acceptance into the city's elite social echelon. During the hotel's heyday, over sixty families listed in *The Blue Blood of New York Society*, a competing publication, also called The Barclay home.

For almost twenty years Mike Vanderbilt enjoyed this rarified environment. It became the setting for one of his most cherished memories. He got married at The Barclay in 1933. He and his fiancée, Gertrude "Gertie" Lewis Conaway, chose to have a small, simple ceremony in the apartment officiated by the Reverend Paul Stevens from St. Thomas Church Fifth Avenue.

The very private 49-year-old groom and his 32-year-old bride never announced their engagement, so the marriage came as a surprise even to those close to the couple. They acquired their marriage license in secret and didn't publicly reveal the union until they were already sailing on their honeymoon. Conaway was described by her society friends as "charming and very attractive," a contrast to Vanderbilt who was often deemed friendly and warm but also quiet and shy. "If he makes as good a husband as he does a bridge partner, it'll be a perfect match," remarked Ely Culbertson, Vanderbilt's friend (and fellow world champion bridge player).

The newlyweds used The Barclay as their city home, and it also served as a convenient perch to Vanderbilt's offices at New York Central. After receiving both his undergraduate and law degrees from Harvard University, he launched his career as a legal assistant at the family-owned company and three years later was elected to a directorship, succeeding J. P. Morgan.

In a magazine profile of Vanderbilt, journalist George Plimpton described him as, "a tall man (6 feet 3 inches in height), impeccably dressed, and his walk a slight indication of his character—brisk, a long arm swing, and toes turned out in strides that seem short and quick for his height, an aggressive walk that carries him a foot or two in advance of any walking partner. What, then, is the Vanderbilt X quality? Obviously, such a quality is an amalgamation of many factors, chief among them what Vanderbilt himself called 'the instinct to excel,' inherited perhaps from his great-grandfather, the

Mike Vanderbilt used the rooftop space inside the top row of windows as a private gymnasium connected to his seventeen-room duplex apartment. It was later converted into storage space for The Barclay.

Commodore." Vanderbilt's life story, Plimpton wrote, was one of "wealth and wit and sportsmanship."

As a top executive at the largest railroad company in the country, Vanderbilt had *New York Central 3*, or *NYC-3* for short, an elegantly festooned private railroad car outfitted for his personal office. It went into service along with three other sister cars commissioned by the railroad in 1928. *NYC-3* was the most lavish of the cars, even boasting a large brick fireplace built into its full service dining room. When Vanderbilt started traveling aboard *NYC-3*, the New York Central System was at the peak of its power, boasting 11,500 road miles of track in the Northeast, Middle Atlantic States, Great Lakes and Canada.

NYC-3 is currently owned by the private corporation VarChandra, which was founded for the express purpose of preserving the famous railroad car. It hopes to keep the car in as pristine condition as possible and consistent with current railway requirements because it still operates as part of a private charter train service.

Photo courtesy of Roger Sramek

In a 1956 Sports Illustrated *article, George Plimpton described Mike Vanderbilt as a "sailor extraordinaire." This replica of a Vanderbilt M-Class racing yacht still sails after fifty years.*

Lovett R. Smith III is VarChandra's president and principal owner, and as is so often the case in firms of this nature, the name is a condensing of his daughters' names, Varina and Chandra. Smith does quite sound like a gentleman of the old stamp who would be very much after the heart of Vanderbilt. Indeed, had he been around at the time, it's certain he'd have been invited to a bridge match or two at one of the Vanderbilt Manhattan manses. It's clear that *NYC-3* could not have fallen into more capable and caring hands.

Although he could literally travel the country and never leave his office, company business was not Vanderbilt's passion. He was more interested in yachting, a hobby passed down from his father and grandfather. He won the America's Cup international yachting title three times, which earned him the cover of *Time* magazine in 1930.

Vanderbilt's immersion into every aspect of sailing is evident in his perfectly designed M-Class boat named *Avatar* (now called

Pursuit), which he commissioned in in the 1930s from William Starling Burgess, one of America's premier yacht designers and naval architects. Few of the original M-boats still exist. Roger Sramek, member of the Corinthian Yacht Club in Sausalito, has sailed on an exact replica of *Pursuit* with Ron MacAnnan, who has owned and maintained her for over fifty years. "She is a real thrill to sail," Sramek enthuses. "*Pursuit* was immediate predecessor to the first J-boats used by Vanderbilt in those early America's Cup races. Sailing out of the Golden Gate on a breezy day, one experiences the risks—tending those running back-stays!—and rewards as Vanderbilt and his crews must have done!" Vanderbilt left an indelible contribution to the sport with his racing victories as well as supporting innovations in boat design.

Conaway shared her husband's passion for sailing. In 1934, after Vanderbilt convinced the racing committee to break with long-standing restrictions, she became the first full-fledged female crew member to compete in an America's Cup race.

The Vanderbilts spent much of their free time in New York playing bridge and entertaining friends. Vanderbilt is credited with inventing the game of contract bridge in the mid-1920s. He was usually at a local bridge club by 4:30 in the afternoon and could easily play until the early hours of the morning, often starting just "one more hand" before rushing out at 2 or 3 a.m., hopping on the *NYC-3*, and barreling towards a business meeting in another city. As the couple spent more time traveling the world on their boats and less time in New York, they gave up their apartment at The Barclay.

When Vanderbilt lost a protracted, headline-making proxy battle for control of New York Central in 1954, he resigned from the company. His departure after forty years at the company signified the end of the Vanderbilt family's active involvement with the company founded by the Commodore in 1864.

NYC-3 Rolls by Ward Morehouse III

For a couple hours I felt like—not a king—but a Vanderbilt ... Harold S. Vanderbilt. Riding the subway to Queens Plaza then hailing a cab to the mammoth "Sunnyside" rail yards where Amtrak trains are sidetracked waiting their next assignments, I found my goal: two lonely private railcars. One is owned by a Texas oil man, the other, NYC-3, by Lovett Smith and colleagues for rail charter. NYC-3 was commissioned in 1928 by its owner, Harold Stirling Vanderbilt, scion of the Vanderbilt family and one of the richest men in the world at the time.

Lovett warmly greets me as I climb aboard but there isn't much time for small talk as he furiously vacuums the dining room of the private railcar to get ready for the trip to Penn Station where he will pick up passengers for a "day trip" to Pittsburgh. After all I had read of Vanderbilt mansions, including the Addison Mizner-designed "El Solando" in Palm Beach which John Lennon once owned, I was impressed not by the grandeur but the simplicity of the car. Sure, it had a dining room as big as some New York City studio apartments. But that's where any sense of ostentation ended. A long mahogany table around which a dinner party for twelve could comfortably gather was the room's main feature, along with old photos of steam engines of yore. Moreover, NYC-3's four bedrooms were anything but grand, the largest big enough for a queen-sized bed, night table and nothing more. Part of this simplicity was that Vanderbilt, a longtime director of the New York Central Railroad, used the car as his "rolling" office for meetings—much to the contraryof any image of the American stage stars of the late nineteenth century whose private cars were veritable palaces.

Photo courtesy of Lovett R. Smith III

As the tail end of an empty Amtrak passenger train "couples" to *NYC-3*, there's a slight, almost gentle jolt and off we go the ten miles or so to Penn Station. The ride is smooth and uneventful other than my own feeling that *this* is really the way to go to Penn Station, especially with a cup of exquisitely-brewed coffee in your hand. I silently toast to Harold Stirling Vanderbilt: yachtsman, railroad executive, and fellow hotel connoisseur. A few minutes later I walk up the stairs from the Penn Station platform and disappear into the crowd on the subway

Photo Courtesy of Caswell-Massey

The classic elegance of New York City's flagship Caswell-Massey store at The Barclay inspired one East Side dowager to reveal to owner Ralph Taylor, "To me Caswell-Massey is a way of life."

Caswell-Massey: Chemists to the Stars

The twelve-year-old boy felt lucky to work in such glamorous surroundings. The carved English walnut cabinets filled with antique apothecary jars nearly reached the ceiling. Victorian crystal chandeliers reflected off the glass-enclosed cases displaying bathtub thermometers, shaving cream, boar bristle brushes, potpourri, soaps made of seaweed, plums, or peaches, and over forty different fragrant oils including lavender, lilac, pine, and frankincense. Although young Ralph Taylor was relegated to sweeping floors and running errands for Caswell-Massey's flagship store located off the lobby of The Barclay, he became entranced by the business. By age sixteen he advanced to bottle washer and by age 33 bought the entire company with his brother Milton.

When The Barclay opened in 1926, it aimed to offer its guests and residents every comfort of home. One of the ways to provide such service was to offer high-end retail in the hotel's public spaces. Caswell-Massey, one of the oldest continually operating businesses in the country, fit perfectly into The Barclay's traditional American style. It traced its lineage to an eighteenth century apothecary that claimed George Washington as a customer. The company spent $80,000 (over $1 million today) to outfit its shop on the corner of Lexington Avenue and 48th Street into a showplace with Old World charm. The store sold medicines from its pharmacy, perfume and toiletries from its counters, and confections from its soda fountain to hotel guests and visitors and neighborhood residents.

In the 1920s drugstore soda fountains were cultural mainstays.

Caswell-Massey's soda fountain served ice cream sodas, sundaes, and banana splits for almost thirty years. An ice cream soda at the time The Barclay opened in 1926 cost about $0.15.

Pharmacists initially used them to sell herbal health or medicinal drinks and sweet sodas to help counteract the taste of bitter medicines. They quickly grew in popularity as a place to grab a quick bite to eat, share a soda, or indulge in a hot fudge sundae. Caswell-Massey's soda fountain offered guests at The Barclay a casual and gracious hangout to socialize with friends and meet local residents. It also attracted a bevy of famous customers.

While Ralph Taylor worked behind the fountain, he served many legendary icons such as movie star Judy Garland, aviation pioneer Amelia Earhart, and actor Lawrence Olivier. Writer Anita Loos and "First Lady of the American stage" Helen Hayes, colleagues and friends, came to the store together to shop and chat over sodas. Loos was also on hand in 1952 as Caswell-Massey celebrated its 200th anniversary by offering free ice cream sodas, champagne, and

Greta Garbo lived among many artists and literati within several blocks of The Barclay. Garbo, along with fellow acting luminary Katharine Hepburn, frequently shopped at the Caswell- Massey flagship store on the first floor of the hotel.

highballs from the soda fountain to go with birthday cake served to over four hundred guests crammed into the store. And the

Photo Courtesy of Caswell-Massey

fountain was a favored meeting spot for Mary Martin and Ezio Pinza when they needed a break from co-starring in Broadway's long-running smash musical *South Pacific*. In the mid-1950s, shortly after the milestone birthday celebration, Caswell-Massey removed the beautiful wood-carved fountain to focus on its retail operations.

The store's massive mirrors continued to reflect well-known faces throughout the years. The notoriously private film idol Greta Garbo lived nearby on 52nd Street for almost four decades. She liked to take long walks around the neighborhood and regularly stopped into the shop. Each time she came, she would purchase a tortoise shell comb. After the actress died, her family came to Caswell-Massey with boxes of unopened packages. It seems Garbo felt compelled to buy something each time she visited the store but could not possibly use all those combs. Another Hollywood power-player, Katharine Hepburn, lived even closer to the hotel. She would dash over from her brownstone on 49th Street to use Caswell-Massey as her corner drugstore.

Ralph and Milton Taylor sold the business in the 1980s and the flagship store closed in 2010. Caswell-Massey provided guests of The Barclay with more than what author John Berendt once described in *Cosmopolitan* magazine as a "functioning historical museum of the apothecary arts." It offered them a connection to both American tradition and neighborhood camaraderie.

Perle Mesta charms future President and First Lady John F. and Jacqueline Kennedy with her infectious humor and unfailing hospitality at one of her infamous parties in 1956.

"The Hostess with the Mostest!"

I've a great big bar and good caviar;
Yes, the best that can be found.
And a large amount in my bank account
When election time comes round.
If you're feeling presidential
You can make it, yes indeed.
There are just three things essential
Let me tell you, all you need.
Is an ounce of wisdom and a pound of gall.
And the hostess with the mostest on the ball.
　　　　　　　　　　　　　　–Irving Berlin

Perle Mesta gave great parties. These Irving Berlin lyrics were a tribute to the Hostess with the Mostest from *Call Me Madam*, a musical based on her life story and a hit of the 1950 Broadway season. Parties defined Mesta, made her political career, and set the standard for entertaining of the era. She threw these legendary and influential extravaganzas wherever she spent her time and fortune mixing with the power set—Washington, D.C., Newport, Palm Beach, and New York. During the late 1920s, this included her apartment at The Barclay. It covered an entire floor and was the largest suite in the hotel.

William Skirvin tried his hand at several businesses before he struck it rich in oil. This provided his daughter Perle with a privileged childhood filled with ponies, poodles, travel, and social training. In her mid-twenties, Mesta, an aspiring singer, moved to New York from her home state of Oklahoma to study music. While there she met and married George Mesta, founder of Mesta Machine Company, a manufacturer of steel mill equipment and machinery in Pittsburgh. George died less than a decade later. In 1925, 36-year-old Mesta was the only heir to her husband's $78 million fortune—the equivalent of over $1 billion today. After her father died, she added even more millions to her net worth.

Mesta became more involved with politics, social issues, and entertaining for enjoyment, networking, and as a way to stay connected to the social set. It made sense for her to choose The Barclay for one of her lengthy stays in New York. She was used to luxurious hotel living. For part of her childhood, she lived in her father's Skirvin Hotel in Oklahoma City, and as a newlywed, she and her husband kept a four-room suite at The Willard Hotel in Washington, D.C.

It was during Mesta's stay at The Barclay that she became well-known for her elaborate parties. Part of this was due to her connection with the Metropolitan Opera. Although she only ever gave one concert of her own, Mesta remained devoted to and a patron of the arts.

In her autobiography *Perle: My Story*, Mesta tells of her relationship to the opera and its stars:

"Rosa Ponselle became one of my dearest friends & It was always fun to go to her apartment and have some of the delicious Italian food she cooked so well. Rosa led a Bohemian life and always had an assortment of characters around her. And I gained a vicarious satisfaction for the career I never had by sitting in on Metropolitan Opera rehearsals and sometimes watching from the wings.

"During this period, I had a large apartment at the Barclay Hotel in New York, and my Metropolitan friends came and kept bringing more and more of their friends. My apartment soon became a well-known hangout for the Metropolitan Opera crowd. I guess you could call that my operatic period. I had Box No. 5 for every Monday night during the Metropolitan season for fifteen years."

Some of the parties were too large even for Mesta's suite of rooms. When she needed more space, she'd rent out a restaurant or ballroom. Since The Barclay aimed to maintain an exclusive, residen-

A 1926 advertisement for The Barclay shows the scale of the neighborhood at the time it was built, including The Park Lane Hotel on the left. Note the telephone number of the sales office. The VAN exchange stands for Vanderbilt.

tial atmosphere, it did not offer ballrooms for large social functions. The Park Lane Hotel, next door to The Barclay on 48th Street, did. According to author James Potter, The Park Lane took a page from the hospitality script of renowned hotelier George Boldt. Boldt, who partly owned The Waldorf-Astoria when it was located where the Empire State Building is today, used to completely change the decor of a room to please his special clients.

Mesta used one of these ballrooms at The Park Lane when she invited a hundred guests—opera superstars Ezio Pinza and Antonio Scotti among them—to celebrate Rosa Ponselle's 1927 groundbreaking performance in the Metropolitan's production of *Norma*. (Ponselle's rendition received such acclaim there is a statue of her as the character in Times Square.)

Mesta did not return to her apartment at The Barclay until 6 a.m. the next morning. It was the most expensive party she'd ever given. Ponselle spent much time at the hotel visiting with Mesta and attending her get-togethers. The two remained friends throughout their lives.

Mesta often mixed her political contacts from Washington with her cultural clique from New York. She created such a convivial, relaxed environment, she could convince guests to let loose and entertain each other. A guest might expect Judy Garland to sing until 3 a.m. but probably did not anticipate hearing Harry Truman play the piano, Dwight D. Eisenhower sing "Drink to Me Only With Thine Eyes," or Alice Vanderbilt (wife of Cornelius II) whistle a duet.

Mesta's political support and prowess paid off in 1949 when she was named the first ambassador to Luxembourg. She was only the third American woman ever appointed to a foreign diplomatic post.

On Mesta's first morning in Luxembourg, a member of the staff asked how she preferred to be addressed. "You can call me madam minister as long as I am representing the United States Government," she answered. The line got repeated as "Call Me Madam" and was widely reported in the press, eventually becoming the title for the Broadway musical.

Legendary theatrical producer and director Hal Prince worked as the casting director for the show (he was drafted into the Korean War and had to give up plans to also be the stage manager). He remembers a later exchange with Mesta that sheds some light on her personality:

"I believe she saw *A Funny Thing Happened on the Way to the Forum* at the National Theatre in Washington and sent me a message that essentially said, 'Shame on you.' It was not vitriolic. I had met her at my mother's apartment some years earlier and she was quite friendly. But she and, apparently, the whole of Washington society, deplored that show. It's a nice anecdote to share and, obviously, we had the last laugh."

That show won several Tony Awards, including one for Prince as Best Producer. The satirical comedy *Call Me Madam* also won four coveted Tony Awards. Mesta loved Ethel Merman's depiction of her on the stage so much she added the actress to the guest lists for her parties. Audiences loved it, too. It ran for two years and spawned numerous touring companies. Broadway impresario George Abbott directed both the stage and film versions of the show. Another play about Mesta's life aired on a 1957 episode of CBS's *Playhouse 90*. Mesta even had a walk-on role. She reveled in the attention.

The show remained popular in revivals. Writing in 1965, for a "Broadway After Dark" column that appeared in the Newhouse Newspapers, the late drama critic Ward Morehouse (and the father of the co-author of this book) interviewed *Call Me Madam* co-author Russell Crouse. "We've kept the book current through the years," Crouse said. "The show has been popular in summer stock. Now we've brought it up to President Lyndon Johnson. We'll refer to some things that have happened in his administration, and Ethel Merman (the star of the original production on Broadway) will give away ten-gallon hats. We'll keep changing it if there are developments that we can kid."

After Mesta left Luxembourg, she regained her "hostess with the mostest" mantle in Washington. Over the next twenty years, she continued to mix presidents, politicians from both sides of the aisle and each side of contentious debates, performers, soldiers, artists, and foreign heads of state at soirees stoked with sumptuous food and wines (though Mesta only drank Coca-Cola since she was a lifelong teetotaler). "I like to mix people, the uppers, the middles and the lowers, the sours and the sweets," she explained in her autobiography. "If there are too many dull ones, I put some aside for the next occasion." Mesta once claimed that a successful party is the combination of cool guests, hot food, cool music, and a warm hostess.

She remained socially active until her death at age 83. At one of her last parties in the early 1970s, Texas politician John Connally toasted her with, "You are a tradition; no, more than a tradition, you are an event in the life of America." Her name remains synonymous with the image of political hostess. Perle Mesta created the benchmark for political entertaining, and The Barclay played a large role in launching this part of her career.

The original ornamental skylight in The Barclay's lobby was created in amber. This current design of clear glass was installed during a later renovation.

Photo Courtesy of Caswell-Massey

The intersection of 48th Street and Lexington Avenue in the 1940s. The man holding a newspaper looks into the Caswell-Massey storefront on the ground floor of The Barclay.

The Barclay Through World War II

After the great optimism and expanding economy of the Roaring Twenties, New Yorkers struggled through the greatest economic crisis of the century, the Great Depression. The stock market crash of 1929 reverberated throughout the 1930s. The exclamation "What will they think of next?" turned into "Brother, Can You Spare a Dime?" Few in the city remained unaffected. Breadlines to feed hungry residents grew longer by the month. Makeshift homeless encampments sprung up in Central Park and along the East and Hudson Rivers. Some industries faced upwards of fifty percent unemployment, manufacturing and construction nearly stopped, and stock prices dropped close to 89 percent. Parks closed, rent strikes broke out, and political demonstrations erupted.

Paradoxically, Depression-era New York was also filled with the glamour and excesses of café society. There was a huge disparity in the lifestyles of the average New Yorker and the social elite. One out of four workers nationwide, close to fifteen million people, were jobless. However, those who "had it," who held on to their wealth despite the economic downturn, continued to live lavishly. Fashion icon Diana Vreeland writes in her autobiography *D.V.*, "It was still a very opulent time in New York." Some of her closest friends such as businessman and diplomat Averell Harriman and Sonny Vanderbilt Whitney (the Commodore's great-great grandson) "and his divine wife, Marie" were "money-in-the-bank rich, not stockbrokers—and everyone dressed for dinner." These so-called beautiful people gathered in fashionable cafés, held lavish parties, and determined what was culturally and socially chic.

Once alcohol consumption became legal again in December 1933, hotels across the city saw a short-term bump in revenue from liquor sales. The opening of a café designed by noted architect John A. Walquist became the focal point for The Barclay's New Year's Eve celebration that year. But the decade-long crisis proved too much for the hotel. Even the lure of liquor and consistent support from the social elite could not maintain the business. The Barclay Park Corporation filed for bankruptcy in 1937.

The New York Central Railroad took control of The Barclay. It managed the hotel under its subsidiary, The New York State Realty and Terminal Company, which also operated several other hotels built on company-owned land such as The Biltmore and The Park Lane. Although federal New Deal programs helped ease the worst effects of the Depression on the city, it took World War II to jumpstart both New York and The Barclay's economic comeback.

The war boom attracted military, government, and business travelers as well as new residents into the city. The resulting housing shortage provided The Barclay with the guests that it needed to generate a revival. The hotel also became a bastion of patriotism in support of the war effort.

Management opened a recreation center for servicemen off of its main lobby to give soldiers and sailors stationed in New York or passing through Grand Central Terminal a convenient and comfortable place to write letters home, listen to music, read, enjoy a cup of coffee and a snack, get directions and advice on navigating the city, or take a well-needed nap. The city issued The Barclay a commendation for its efforts to address the needs and keep up the morale of the troops.

The hotel also relied on its newly revamped cuisine to show its support for the servicemen. During the 1940s, The Barclay was praised by both trade journals and general periodicals for the signature dishes developed by its newly hired French chefs. "Filet of Sole Barclay" was an especially popular recipe reprinted in news-

The Barclay Through World War II

papers and magazines. Despite the name, it also included oysters deep fried in lard and wrapped in bacon. The dining room served a modified version of the dish on "meatless" Tuesdays and Fridays instituted by management in order to comply with the food rationing established by the wartime Office of Price Administration.

The Barclay offered servicemen the chance to experience the chef's special dishes for the holidays. Throughout the war, they were treated to free meals in order to make celebrations away from home and family as festive as possible. The public could join them for a full, gourmet turkey dinner at the regular price of $3.50 (at a time when a hotel room rented for about $15 a night).

The Barclay's housekeeping department joined in the wartime encouragement of the troops. They began to collect gifts of candy like the popular Oh Henry! bars, books, magazines, cigarettes, and clothing to create care packages for the men serving overseas. Their generosity was not only appreciated by the men who received them but encouraged and added to by hotel guests and noted with gratitude by the families of the men fighting at the front.

That same department later turned into a makeshift animal sanctuary for a refugee from one of the most memorable features from this era of The Barclay. "Meet me at the birdcage!" became a popular refrain for New Yorkers gathering for Midtown dinner, drinks, or theatre dates. The distinctive fourteen-foot high birdcage, the centerpiece of The Barclay's lobby for decades, was installed in the 1940s. The bronze cage held as many as a dozen exotic birds (yellow albino cockatiels, red-crested cardinals, German warblers...) at one time. Guests not wanting to leave their own birds at home could house them along with the flock.

Children jockeyed for seats on the circular leather couch later installed around the aviary. *New York Times* reporter David Dunlap wrote about his first trip to the Big Apple as a kid in the 1960s: "What does a 9-year-old boy see when he comes to New York for the first time? How does he feel? What images will he keep from his visit

Photo Courtesy of Rose Billings

The Turtle Bay neighborhood adjacent to Terminal City transformed from tenements and rooming houses into a community known for its gracious brownstones and lush gardens in the early 1920s. At the time The Barclay opened, a five-story brownstone sold for around $50,000.

for the rest of his life? Song birds in the lobby of the Barclay Hotel." While the whole city impressed Dunlap enough that he made it his home as an adult, the birds created a vital and vivid memory.

The birds also created a problem. Some of them didn't get along with each other. The hotel staff started keeping one of the birds separated for its own safety because the others continually pecked at it. Once removed from the bullies, he sat happily and calmly on a perch in housekeeping. Perhaps he was shrewder than everyone imagined and just wanted a single room.

The music and frivolity of the birdcage ushered in a new sense of style to The Barclay. Gone were the sedate colonial designs that gave the feeling of lounging with George Washington at Mount Vernon. An impression of fun, experimentation, and openness to the public replaced R. T. H. Halsey and Pauline Sabin's plans for cultured exclusivity.

The streets around The Barclay also made a cultural shift. The hotel sits on the western fringe of Manhattan's Turtle Bay neighborhood. Once the sole purview of upper crust socialites, the 1940s ushered in a wave of more artistic residents. In particular, a series of brownstones on 49th Street called Turtle Bay Gardens, a little more than a block east of The Barclay, became home to creative luminaries such as Broadway composer Stephen Sondheim, actor Tyrone Power, conductor Leopold Stokowski, and author Kurt Vonnegut. Katharine Hepburn lived in one of these brownstones for more than sixty years, and staff members recall watching her determined stride as she frequently passed by and through the hotel. Artist Georgia O'Keeffe and her husband, photographer Alfred Stieglitz, were even closer neighbors to The Barclay, living at the Hotel Shelton directly across Lexington Avenue for nearly ten years. It is fitting that two of the most famous writers in the twentieth century chose this environment to pursue their work.

Ernest Hemingway sits on a dock next to his fishing boat Pilar. Not only a nickname for Hemingway's second wife Pauline, "Pilar" is the name of the heroine in For Whom the Bell Tolls.

8

Papa Hemingway and the Forties

Ernest Hemingway, the famed author and journalist known for drinking hard, seeking adventure, courting danger, and generally living large, created a temporary home and writing studio at The Barclay.

During the 1930s, Hemingway traveled to Spain to cover its civil war as a reporter for the North American Newspaper Alliance. He was accompanied by Martha Gellhorn, his new love interest and a fellow journalist. While Hemingway spent much of his time carousing with ex-patriots from various countries there to report on the war, aid in the fighting, or manage the international politics of the conflict, he witnessed enough of the war to use its brutal reality as the basis for one of his most acclaimed novels, *For Whom the Bell Tolls*. The book follows an American explosives expert who works with guerrilla forces against Francisco Franco's fascist regime.

In the summer of 1940 Hemingway and Gellhorn (who would soon become his third wife) checked into The Barclay. The 41-year-old author was in New York to work with literary editor Max Perkins at Charles Scribner's Sons. They were rushing to get the galleys of *For Whom the Bell Tolls* to the printer in time for an October release date.

It proved to be a particularly hot summer, with a severe drought and heat wave that killed hundreds across the country. New York's concrete jungle did little to alleviate the heat, especially as few buildings and homes had yet to install air-conditioning. The Barclay was no exception and Hemingway sweated his way through 96-hour writing stints with only an electric fan to blow the increasingly hot air around the stuffy room. He was reading and revising up to 300 pages of copy a day to complete the final draft.

Hemingway hated to be alone when he stopped writing. After intense stretches of productivity, he would invite friends up to his room to relax, drink, and talk. Robert Van Gelder, a reporter for *The New York Times*, witnessed one of these get-togethers as he interviewed the author for an article titled, "Ernest Hemingway Talks of Work and War."

Van Gelder watched Hemingway, dressed in an open pajama top, hold court with a rotating group of acquaintances, including Gustavo Duran. Hemingway revealed that the former pianist and composer, who commanded Loyalist troops in Spain's Civil War, was a character in the new novel. Hemingway wanted to ask Duran questions to make sure what he wrote about in the book rang true. Throughout the evening a fifth of Scotch and bowl of ice sat within easy arm's reach of the boisterous group. The telephone rang almost constantly.

Van Gelder noted: "After his long session of work Hemingway looked elephant-big, enormously healthy. His talk is unevenly paced, a quick spate and then a slow search for a word. His chair keeps hitching across the floor toward the other chairs, and then as he reaches a point, a conclusion, he shoves his chair back to the edge of the group again."

Hemingway left a signed copy of his book contract on top of his hotel room dresser. It showed the author's royalties at fifteen percent on the first 25,000 copies sold and twenty percent for every copy after that. It was an unusually high rate for an author and reflected Hemingway's popularity at the time. He was the most widely read male author in America. *For Whom the Bell Tolls* sold over half a million copies within months of its release.

Hemingway seldom left his room at The Barclay. As soon as he finished the revisions, they were sent to the printer, who rushed to set the galleys. The book would hit store shelves in less than three months. As soon as the revisions were complete, Hemingway set off for home in Cuba, where Gellhorn had traveled ahead and was waiting for him. *For Whom the Bell Tolls* became one of Hemingway's greatest commercial and critical triumphs. It was nominated for—but famously and controversially denied—the 1941 Pulitzer Prize for Literature. Although the selection committee and board agreed to award the book its top honor, the president of the board, Nicholas Murray Butler, found Hemingway's story offensive and overruled the choice. No award for fiction was given that year. *For Whom the Bell Tolls* was made into a film starring Gary Cooper and Ingrid Bergman two years later. It was nominated for nine Academy Awards including Best Picture.

Although *Gone With the Wind* producer David O. Selznick also frequented The Barclay when he was in New York, he fortunately did not run into Hemingway. The two men did not get along.

As A. E. Hotchner tells it in *Papa Hemingway*, his biography of the writer, Hemingway got a telegram from Selznick during one of his trips to Spain: "Selznick, who had just completed a remake of *A Farewell to Arms* with his wife Jennifer Jones. . . had not paid Ernest anything for this version because back in the Twenties the book had been sold outright with no provision for remakes. This telegram said that Selznick had just informed the world press that although not legally obligated to, he was hereby pledging himself to pay Mr. Hemingway fifty thousand dollars from the profits of the picture, if and when it earned any profits.

"Ernest, who had never kept secret his lack of affection for Mr. Selznick, dictated a telegram in reply saying that if by some miracle, Selznick's movie, which starred 41-year-old Mrs. Selznick [Jennifer Jones] portraying 24-year-old Catherine Barkley, did earn $50,000, Selznick should have all the money changed into nickels at his local bank and shove them up his [explicative deleted!] untill they came out of his ears."

As far as we know, there is no connection between the fictional Ms. Barkley and The Barclay Hotel.

Eugene O'Neill by noted photographer Alice Boughton, known for her portraits of New York's prominent literary and theatre figures. One of Boughton's mentors was pioneering photographer Alfred Stieglitz, who lived across the street from The Barclay for over a decade.

The Iceman Cometh to The Barclay

In the fall of 1945, American playwright Eugene O'Neill still showed signs of several recurrent illnesses which sapped his strength and left him unable to write for many years. His hands trembled violently. This left him unable to hold a pen and, since he was reluctant to turn to a typewriter or dictation to compose his plays, interfered with his creative process. Several doctors misdiagnosed the rare, degenerative neurological disorder (later identified as cerebellar cortical atrophy), but the effect on the writer's work was more important to him than giving the incurable problem a name.

It was left to his wife, former actress Carlotta Monterey, to make arrangements to move from their current home on the west coast into an eighth-floor suite at The Barclay. Although O'Neill had not been writing, he had been planning to produce one of his existing plays after World War II came to an end. He was aware that the tense cultural climate of wartime was not the right atmosphere for his introspective, somber, and pessimistic dramas. But by late 1945 O'Neill felt that both he and the audience were ready to tackle new challenges.

Life at The Barclay suited the famed writer. At this point in his career, the 57-year-old had already won three Pulitzer Prizes for Drama and a Nobel Prize for Literature. Within a few weeks of living at the hotel, O'Neill started to regain his health enough to work on final revisions of the Broadway-bound play *The Iceman Cometh*, often considered his most intricate and certainly one of his most widely analyzed works.

Although O'Neill wrote the play in less than six months during the summer and fall of 1939, it did not premiere on stage until October 1946. The show would be mounted again a decade later for a highly acclaimed Off-Broadway production starring Jason Robards that solidified its reputation as a dramatic masterpiece. Three more Broadway revivals, TV and film versions, and sell-out performances with stars Nathan Lane and Brian Dennehy in a 2012 Chicago theatre production are testament to the play's enduring significance to the theatre community and audiences alike.

In their definitive biography of O'Neill, Arthur and Barbara Gelb describe this brief interlude in the playwright's wildly peripatetic life. They quote Lawrence Langer, O'Neill's longtime friend and a founder of the Theatre Guild—the company producing *The Iceman Cometh*—as saying, "He enjoyed his visits to the Guild every afternoon and he began to put his manuscript into final shape. We all felt the fact that he was at work again in the theatre was doing wonders in bringing him back to his health."

O'Neill also felt well enough while at The Barclay to spend time with friends and colleagues. He and Carlotta regularly entertained in their suite. According to the Gelbs, theatre and film producer Max Gordon (immortalized in Cole Porter's song "Anything Goes") regaled O'Neill with stories from his varied career. He once went on a three-hour binge repeating jokes, songs, and bawdy ditties told to him by composer and performer George M. Cohan. Gordon remembered that O'Neill enjoyed himself so much that the songs "almost lifted him out of his seat." Cohan starred in O'Neill's *Ah, Wilderness*, his only comedy, when it opened on Broadway in 1933.

The writer also enjoyed reminiscing in his rooms with Walter Casey, a childhood friend who now worked in the city as a freelance writer, and with Richard Weeks, a Princeton University classmate during O'Neill's one rebellious, rowdy year of college. "Gene was lawless, as far as the university was concerned," Weeks later recalled to O'Neill's biographers. The gatherings at the hotel were considerably tamer but no less enjoyable for the old friends.

In a great departure for the previously ill author, he used his Midtown location as a base to explore New York's attractions. O'Neill went to ball games, prizefights, and movies. He rented limos to venture out of the city to bet at the racetracks. He spent afternoons with Lawrence Langner. And he spent many evenings with Winfield Aronberg, his attorney and "jazz around pal." The two men frequented jazz clubs up and down 52nd Street, a lively stretch between Fifth and Seventh Avenues renowned for hosting music legends such as Charlie Parker, Thelonious Monk, and Louis Prima from the 1930s through the early 1950s.

O'Neill also used The Barclay as a space to reconnect with his sons. O'Neill's relationship with his children was strained at best. He had recently cut off all communication with his only daughter, Oona. The beautiful teenager inspired many admirers as one of the most sought-after debutantes in New York. But the man she fell in love with found his fame and fortune in Hollywood. As soon as Oona turned eighteen, she married screen legend Charlie Chaplin, almost forty years her senior. O'Neill disapproved and never spoke to his daughter again.

But he and Carlotta did host many dinners for his two sons, both of whom lived in New York at that time. O'Neill's oldest son, Eugene Jr., who enjoyed the closest relationship of the three siblings to their father, visited the suite for long talks and watching the television Carlotta purchased for their rooms. Eugene was a classics scholar with a tumultuous personal life, much like his father's. It was partly due to respect for the junior Eugene's wishes that O'Neill put a stipulation on his manuscript for *Long Day's Journey Into Night*. The author delivered it to Random House the month after he checked into The Barclay. But he insisted that the publisher not release the script until twenty-five years after his death. The autobiographical play revealed too many painful family truths for both Eugenes. (Carlotta released the play in 1956 after the men died. It won O'Neill another Pulitzer Prize, this one posthumously.)

O'Neill also had a somewhat shy and awkward reunion with his younger son Shane at The Barclay. They had not seen each other in five years. But Shane soon returned to the suite to introduce his father to his wife Cathy. "My immediate impression of him," Cathy later remarked, "was that here was a very elegant man. I'd sort of expected the old sailor, the saloon guy I had read about. He was extremely well dressed and had an Old World air about him. He was very gallant, had beautiful manners." The hotel hosted the last, brief respite from tension the father and son would share.

In the spring of 1946, the O'Neills moved out of The Barclay and into a penthouse apartment on the Upper East Side. The playwright jumped into the whirlwind of preparing and casting *The Iceman Cometh*. Excitement over the show earned O'Neill the cover of *Time* magazine. He would not live to see any more of his plays produced on Broadway.

The months O'Neill spent at The Barclay were part of the playwright's last great burst of health and energy. He declined rapidly and could no longer enjoy the type of social life he experienced in that last period of living in New York. He and Carlotta left the city and retreated from friends, family, and society before the writer succumbed to his illness in 1953.

Eugene O'Neill, as he succinctly and profanely pointed out on his deathbed, was born in a hotel room and died in a hotel room. As the son of a popular nineteenth-century actor, he came into the world at The Barrett Hotel on Broadway in what is now Times Square. Sixty-four tumultuous years and fifty plays later, he died at The Hotel Shelton in Boston. The time in between that he spent at The Barclay helped produce one of O'Neill's last great literary contributions to society.

The Cornell Club occupied 30,000 square feet on the third floor of The Barclay for over twenty years. This wood-paneled library was a favorite refuge for visiting alumni.

Welcome to the Club

In addition to hosting long-term residents, The Barclay welcomed long-time tenants attracted to the exclusivity of the hotel and its central location. After an increase in the number of men and women attending college in the 1920s, it became more popular in the subsequent decades to set up local or regional alumni clubs for graduates to maintain relationships with their schools and with each other. A group from Cornell University set the trend at The Barclay when it opened a membership-only club in 1939.

The Cornell Club signed a twelve-year lease for the entire third floor of the hotel. The organization hired Cross & Cross, the building's original architects, to renovate thirty thousand square feet of space accessed through a private entrance on 48th Street. The extensive plans called for one main dining room; three smaller private dining rooms; an informal dining area for light lunches and snacks; a library; lounges to relax, read, or catch up with other members; card and billiard rooms; and an area reserved exclusively for women. The private space available for alumni included thirty-nine bedrooms and suites that could be leased for long- or short-term stays. While construction was completed, the club occupied space on the ground floor of the hotel.

Several other schools rented smaller rooms in The Barclay. Bryn Mawr, Mount Holyoake, Smith, and Wellesley Colleges opened clubs to serve alumnae in the city. According to hotel records, Rachel Niles, a member from Wellesley, remembered spending time in the well-appointed club rooms during its time at The Barclay from

Ornamentation, specifically personification like this man's face, is a hallmark of buildings designed by Cross & Cross. Faded lettering still marks the former entrance to the Cornell Club.

1940-1955. She was impressed to find they were furnished with antiques and fine reproductions. "But," she recalled, "it was all very homey." Club activities included lectures, teas, socials, fundraisers, and interviewing prospective students.

When the Cornell Club moved out in 1962, its membership roll had reached a peak of two thousand alumni. Half of the third floor, including most of the public rooms, was taken over by the Manhattan Club in 1966. The private organization appreciated the separate entrance and elevator for many of the city's legal and political elites that belonged to the exclusive club. Club President John L. Flynn had been forced to find a new home when the building it occupied for over 65 years, the Jerome Mansion (named for its original owner Leonard Jerome, one of Cornelius Vanderbilt's business partners), was put up for sale the previous year and slated for possible demolition. Members included Senator Jacob Javits, New York Mayor Abe Beame, Congressman, New York Mayor and Presidential candidate John Lindsay, and generations of the city's and country's influential lawyers, judges, and politicians (including Presidents Grover Cleveland and Franklin Roosevelt).

The Barclay housed another select organization for almost half of a century. From 1958 until the pageant moved from its Atlantic City roots in 2005, the first stop for the newly crowned Miss America was a suite at The Barclay. The contest winner used the hotel as her home base while in New York for television appearances, interviews, and meetings with organization officials. The parade of talented, accomplished women included several Miss Americas who went on to public careers in entertainment or media including actress Mary Ann Mobley, Fox News anchor Gretchen Carlson, veternarian and broadcast journalist Debbye Turner and singer/actress Vanessa Williams who was the first African-American winner.

Nineteen years before Williams's reign, a controversy broke out at The Barclay. Deborah Bryant, newly crowned Miss America 1966, held a press conference at the hotel and reporters asked her about the pageant's inadequate representation of African-American women.

Deborah Bryant poses on The Barclay's rooftop for one of her first photo shoots as Miss America 1966. Her mother, Irene Bryant, also used the hotel as a New York City base when she worked as the full-time chaperone for Deborah's Miss America successor.

Bryant hesitated to answer such a sensitive question. Leonora Slaughter, the contest's director, declared the topic inappropriate since Bryant was Miss America and not the President of the United States. Slaughter escorted Bryant from the room and cancelled the press conference.

The Barclay also became the inadvertent star of a comedy bit between Susan Perkins, Miss America 1978, and host Johnny Carson during her appearance on *The Tonight Show*. When the comedian asked to see the famous rhinestone crown, Perkins first unwrapped it from its traveling case—a towel imprinted with the Barclay Hotel logo. Carson launched into a series of joking questions about how she got the towel and insinuated that she stole it from the hotel. The appearance marked both Perkins's and The Barclay's late night debut. The impromptu banter with the quick-witted host must have been good practice for Perkins, as she later became a successful spokesperson and news reporter.

Many other groups and companies, such as The Association of American University Women and American Steel, have rented office space or held long-standing employee suites at The Barclay. The tradition of using an upscale hotel like The Barclay for a Manhattan headquarters offered top executives a place to stay when in the city for business or to attend a function, entertain visiting clients in a corporate suite, reliable service for events and meetings, and an impressive Midtown address.

By the 1970s, The Barclay–indicated by the arrow–was increasingly dwarfed by modern skyscrapers rising in its Midtown East neighborhood.

The Barclay Through the 1970s

After World War II, New York experienced several boom and bust cycles. In the mid to late 1940s, residents attempted to readjust after four years of wartime instability and disruption. The city looked towards a new era of building, urban renewal, and a consumer economy growing rapidly for the first time since the 1920s. Competing visions of what the city should become by public leaders such as "Master Builder" Robert Moses and architectural and neighborhood activist Jane Jacobs impacted the postwar physical and cultural landscape.

The demolition of large swaths of previously occupied land for redevelopment or the creation of expressways and public projects reshaped the city. Some neighborhoods were literally wiped off the map, but Midtown Manhattan experienced a building boom that left it studded with new glass and steel skyscrapers.

In the early 1950s the architecture and urban fabric of the area around The Barclay started to change dramatically. The Terminal City concept stalled as commerce swept Lexington Avenue virtually clean of residential buildings.

The 24-story Lever House completed in 1952 and 38-story Seagram Building completed in 1958 brought the International Style skyscraper design to The Barclay's East Side neighborhood. Walls of glass and steel replaced brick and limestone. Open spaces and plazas replaced ground floors that occupied entire building lots. These designs helped usher in a new phase of commercial office towers in Midtown. In the next two and a half decades, the skyline would include other signature buildings such as the sleek, sculptural, 39-story United Nations Secretariat building and the pioneering Pan Am (now Met Life), Citicorp and AT&T buildings.

The United Nations Headquarters, based on plans by innovative architects Oscar Niemeyer and Le Corbusier, showcased the International Style skyscraper design but also served as a harbinger of a new wave of globalism in New York. Corporations sought to develop or expand their presence in the city because it was now officially recognized as an influential player on the international stage. The Barclay was in a prime location to service this influx of business and diplomatic travelers.

Henry Cabot Lodge, Jr., former U.S. senator and namesake grandson of the politician from Massachusetts, was appointed the American ambassador to the UN in 1953 and ran for vice president of the U.S. on the ticket with Richard Nixon in 1960. During this period of the politician's career, he used The Barclay as his New York headquarters. No American before or since has come close to equaling Lodge's seven-year term at the UN.

While The Barclay never changed its neo-Federal style to mimic contemporary modernism or globalism, it did inadvertently add to the birth of modern design on a much smaller, but more comfortable, scale than the buildings going up around it. In 1945, George Nelson first saw Charles and Ray Eameses' groundbreaking molded-plywood furniture at a showcase held at The Barclay. The husband-and-wife team from California came to New York hoping to introduce their designs to a new audience. Nelson, design director of the Herman Miller furniture company, offered them a partnership on the spot. The Eameses' work under the company's institutional support would include many iconic modern designs that are now staples in homes, offices, and schools across the world. Herman Miller became one the top furniture companies in the country. Charles and Ray have been heralded as two of the most influential designers of the twentieth century. Much of their work from these collections is still displayed at New York's Museum of Modern Art.

Rooftop view from The Barclay down Lexington Avenue towards the Chrysler Building on 42nd Street. When the Art Deco icon opened in 1930 it was the tallest building in the world. It offered a stark contrast in style to the sedate look of The Barclay's neighborhood.

Despite the innovations and building boom occurring in Midtown, by the late 1960s, New York City faced mounting troubles. Major manufacturing companies relocated to cheaper land outside of the city, changes in shipping methods increased the need for more space than Manhattan's waterfronts could offer, industrial jobs that had long supported its tax base were gone, large-scale construction projects spread city resources thin, a significant drop in federal investments, and suburban flight all contributed to fiscal stagnation and urban decay.

In 1973 New York City Comptroller Abraham Beame wanted a more active role in helping the city regain its economic footing. He decided to run for mayor and established his campaign offices on the third floor of The Barclay. The accountant and former budget director successfully ran on the slogan "He Knows the Buck." Ironically, he ended up leading the city through its worst financial crisis in history. Crime rates skyrocketed, drug traffic bordered on epidemic proportions, schools declined, race riots broke out, municipal layoffs soared, and the largest metropolitan area in the country was in serious jeopardy of going bankrupt.

The city's problems were evident with a single glance around once popular landmarks. Central Park had deteriorated. The landscape became overgrown and several sections—including the well-known Sheep Meadow and Belvedere Castle—were fenced off and deserted. Times Square lost its luster. Many legitimate theatres and businesses closed and the area became overrun with seedy shops and cinemas.

Beame turned to the federal government for help. A famous 1975 *New York Daily News* headline summed up the President's response: "Ford to City: Drop Dead." However, less than a month later Ford relented after being persuaded that New York's demise would have national repercussions.

The Barclay was not immune to these difficulties. In 1968 the Pennsylvania and New York Central Railroads merged into the Penn Central Railroad. But just over two years later, changing freight and passenger transportation trends (a spokesman reported that the *Twentieth Century Limited* from Chicago—deemed the "world's greatest train" at its peak—pulled into Grand Central Terminal with only fifty-five passengers served by more than seventy crew members) and mismanagement forced the new company to declare bankruptcy. It was the largest in U.S. corporate history at that time. As part of the restructuring process, the hotels owned and operated under The New York State Realty and Terminal Company were liquidated along with many of the company's other assets.

Martin Luther King, Jr. photographed at a press conference by Marion S. Trikosko.

Martin Luther King, Jr.: A Conversation for Change

Like the United Nations that opened nearby, The Barclay has been the backdrop of low-key but important international meetings. One such encounter involved two leaders from dramatically different backgrounds who nevertheless found much to share.

Martin Luther King, Jr. was late. A day late to be precise. The cancelled flight from Charlotte, North Carolina, kept him from arriving in time for his meeting at The Barclay. The gathering with Ahmed Ben Bella, Prime Minister of the New Algerian Republic, had been King's suggestion. Luckily, Ben Bella was able to re-arrange his schedule the following day to host the eloquent reverend who at the time was at the forefront of the American Civil Rights Movement. Although their professional and personal paths would take very different courses, the two leaders had much in common. They discovered their similarities in the worldwide struggle to gain human freedom and dignity over the course of the two hours they talked in Ben Bella's suite at The Barclay.

Ben Bella was a freedom fighter instrumental in Algeria's revolt against French colonial rule, even though he was imprisoned for much of the eight-year battle over independence. His March 1962 release had been a high priority for the provisional government during the peace negotiations that ended the war with France. At the time of Ben Bella's meeting with King just seven months later, he served as his country's prime minister and in less than a year would become its first elected president.

King was in the midst of his own multi-year battle for African-American rights and equality. The latest fight occurred twelve days earlier as James Meredith became the first African American to enroll at the University of Mississippi. Riots over this landmark event killed two and injured over a hundred people. President Kennedy sent in 5,000 federal troops to control the violence. Ben Bella knew of the incident and was also aware of the protests and direct action campaigns orchestrated by King and other leaders of the Civil Rights Movement.

In an essay about the meeting called "The Ben Bella Conversation," King wrote, "Ben Bella and I discussed issues ranging from the efficacy of non-violence to the Cuban crisis. However, it was on the question of racial injustice that we spent most of our time." The exchange gave the two leaders a sense of solidarity in their respective crusades. King recalled that, throughout the meeting, Ben Bella repeatedly expressed to him that, "We are brothers."

Ben Bella left The Barclay later that afternoon for Washington, D.C., where he would continue the diplomatic tour he began at the United Nations. The Prime Minister had lunch and a discussion at the White House with President Kennedy. The following day King arrived in the nation's capital to do the very same thing.

Although Ben Bella's political future in Algeria would be fraught with setbacks and disappointments and King faced ongoing struggles in his quest for universal recognition and equality, the tone at the meeting of these two charismatic leaders was one of hope and determination. The Barclay became host to the international exchange of two icons who each challenged and changed the course of their respective nations.

Hollywood legend and style icon Gloria Swanson brought her unique glamour and elegance to The Barclay.

Glitterati

For nearly ninety years, entertainment, sports, diplomatic, and political icons have added a dash of glitz and mystique to the ambiance of The Barclay. The hotel has attracted global superstars as diverse as Mick Jagger, Woody Allen, Tony Bennett, Yoko Ono, Marlon Brando, Billy Crystal, Gladys Knight, Vanessa Redgrave, Denzel Washington, and Ozzie Osbourne. Screen legend Gloria Swanson often visited The Barclay over the span of her six-decade long career. She came out of semi-retirement after her smash success in 1950's *Sunset Boulevard* to act on stage and television. While performing in New York, she chose the hotel in part because of its proximity to the theatres and Midtown studios. Broadcast pioneer Arthur Godfrey kept a suite and aired a show from the Lexington Hotel but chose to relax and socialize across the street in The Barclay's welcoming lobby. The hotel has even become a minor celebrity in its own right. The films *Spiderman 2*, *Taking of Pelham 123*, *The Bitter Pill*, and the TV shows *Sex in the City*, *The Americans*, and NBC News all include scenes or interviews shot at the hotel.

Beloved sports heroes also lent their personal charisma to the atmosphere at The Barclay. In the 1950s, boxing Hall of Famers Rocky Graziano and Floyd Patterson liked to frequent the hotel's dining room before catching a fight at the old Madison Square Garden. The heavyweight champs sat at the same table every time—number 85.

The Gold Room Bar attracted yet another boxing great. A hotel bartender recalled one night in 1959 when he was getting ready to close. As this was around 2 a.m., there was only one customer left, a regular who sat at the bar with his head buried in *The New York Times*. A boiterous group of men showed up and grabbed space at the other end of the counter. The bartender recognized them as members of the New York Rangers hockey team who had developed a reputation for causing trouble and destroying property. One of the men grabbed some peanuts out of a bowl and threw them at the customer quietly reading the paper through thick eyeglasses. It only took one look. Jack Dempsey slowly lowered his paper. The players immediately recognized "The Manassa Mauler," former heavyweight champion of the world, and made a hasty retreat from the hotel.

More recently, when John Calipari coached the men's basketball teams at the University of Memphis and University of Kentucky, he brought his players to the hotel. There was only one wrinkle. Some of the players needed "extensions" to fit their very tall frames into the hotel's regular-sized beds. Alas, the hotel did not have any. It was a crisis of unprecedented size and scope, as it were. The hotel simply doesn't get that many guests in excess of 6'4". No hotel does, except possibly at one time The Pennsylvania, across the street from Madison Square Garden. The Barclay Hotel investigated purchasing such extensions, only to discover that it was simpler to buy a supply of extra-long beds.

On another memorable occasion, when Major League Baseball's All-Star Game was held at Yankee Stadium, the hotel had the honor of playing host to all of the Hall of Famers attending the event. The Barclay's chef made a detailed replica of Yankee Stadium in marzipan for public display. The staff produced a video in which each department sang "Take Me Out to the Ball Game." Excited glances were exchanged as Willie Mays, Bob Feller, and Roger Clemmons crossed through the lobby. When autograph seekers caught sight of pitching great Gaylord Perry, they fluttered outside the front door like locusts. The hotel staff was valiantly holding them at bay, but Perry gallantly spent time with the fans that wanted to meet him.

Even before Bill Clinton developed a national fan base, he added political prestige to The Barclay. When he was running for president in 1992, then-candidate Bill Clinton used the hotel as his New York campaign headquarters. The business of politics operated out of several offices, but Clinton and his wife, future Senator and Secretary of State Hillary Rodham Clinton, also took rooms for their home base while in the city. Their presence ensured vice presidential candidate Al Gore and his wife Tipper and Clinton's mother spent time at the hotel during the campaign.

Clinton was not the only president of the U.S. or head of state to stay at The Barclay. President Ronald Reagan and First Lady Nancy Reagan brought gracious charm and a hint of old Hollywood glamour to the hotel. When one of the presidents of Haiti arrived for his visit, he recognized two staff members he knew from his home country. He happily posed for a photo with them to appear on the front page of a local Haitian newspaper. And when the UN is in session, virtually every guest is an important world leader.

Although The Barclay never courted attention for its ability to attract prominent public figures, the presence of those famous faces and charismatic celebrities lent a sparkle to the refined atmosphere of the hotel.

A 1926 National Hotel Review description of The Barclay as, "Imposing without, palatial within, and handsomely appointed throughout" still fits its grand lobby.

14

Becoming InterContinental

On February 3, 1982, a luncheon to celebrate the 55th anniversary and official reopening of the renovated Barclay Hotel reproduced much of the original 1926 dinner menu—minus the Beluga caviar—for company executives, New York officials, and invited guests. The occasion also marked a name change for the veritable hostelry. It became known as The Hotel InterContinental New York.

After Penn Central declared bankruptcy in 1970, many of its assets were liquidated. The U.S. District Court overseeing the company's reorganization chose to sell The Barclay, Biltmore, and Roosevelt Hotels as one group. After a fierce bidding war, The Loews Corporation won with an offer of $55 million.

Loews quickly resold the remaining "railroad hotels" as individual properties. New York developer Paul Milstein bought The Biltmore and The Roosevelt. In July 1978, InterContinental Hotels Corporation, a subsidiary of Pan American World Airways, acquired The Barclay. Chairman Paul Sheeline stated the company planned to make The Barclay the flagship of its worldwide chain, which, at that point, included eighty hotels. InterContinental was created in 1946 by Juan Trippe, chairman and founder of Pan Am. He anticipated the growing need to accommodate Pan Am passengers taking advantage of world travel in the new era of commercial jets. The first InterContinental hotel opened in Belém, Brazil three years later.

It was the perfect time to buy The Barclay. The area around the hotel bustled with new development attempting to transform it from a predominately business-oriented enclave to include more retail, hotels, and apartments—a venture similar to what Terminal City started over fifty years before. Many of the surrounding monuments to that era were also in the process of renovations or redevelopment. For example, Grand Central Terminal and the Chrysler Building received architectural facelifts and the Abercrombie & Fitch store, Airline Ticket Building, and Shelton Towers apartments were all repurposed.

In 1978 New York's hospitality industry was also experiencing a rejuvenation of sorts. The city's 100,000 hotels were close to ninety percent booked on any given day, their best year in history up to that time. Michael Grosso, executive vice president of the Fifth Avenue Association whose members included top Midtown hotels, made dozens of phone calls a day trying to find desperate travelers an empty room. This was quite a change from the sixty-six percent occupancy rate just seven years earlier.

One turning point for the recently impoverished city came with its prominence in the 1976 Bicentennial Celebration marking the 200th anniversary of the Declaration of Independence. New York planned a comprehensive program including an international flotilla of classic tall ships and an unprecedented display of fireworks over the Statue of Liberty. Art critic and essayist Hilton Kramer described the impact of the public celebrations: "Nothing that took place in a theatre or a museum, nothing we read or heard or looked at, inspired quite the same outpouring of feeling." The activities brought millions of visitors into the struggling city.

A combination of business conventioneers and European tourists attracted by a good currency exchange rate kept the economic momentum building through the late 1970s. And most importantly, an extensive and unforgettable piece of advertising re-branded the city's image. The 1977 "I Love New York" media blitz of TV commercials, radio spots, magazine ads, t-shirts, buttons, and a catchy song delivered by Broadway stars and notable New Yorkers (often painfully but endearingly off-key) kicked off a new era of recovery for the city which was solidified by the Wall Street boom of the 1980s.

The Barclay contributed to this redefinition of the city and the Midtown neighborhood with a $30 million dollar modernization. Fred G. Peelen guided the hotel through this and several other restorations during his nine-year tenure as general manager of The Barclay. He also helped target the new type of clientele the InterContinental hoped to attract.

In his book *A Room with a World View*, James Potter explains that the company's initial organizational model was to meet the needs of corporate travelers in an increasingly global marketplace. The Barclay did court guests seeking to be close to the business and diplomatic hub in Midtown Manhattan. But it still aimed for the upper end of that market.

Copy from a late 1970s advertisement for the hotel shows the type of guest The Barclay pursued during this time: "New York is breakfast with your banker, dinner with your lawyers and trying to keep a hundred securities analysts from having you for lunch." This brings to mind the early ads targeting those guests and residents that "seek the finest."

Peelen was also behind The Barclay's experiment as one of the first hotel teleconferencing centers in the world. Satellite televisions were set up in both The Barclay and the London InterContinental hotels. In the early 1980s, the company spent close to a million dollars to transform accommodations in each hotel into a boardroom studio. The décor included a conference table, wood paneling, and cameras that were so technologically advanced they could clearly pick out a pinhead on the floor. At pre-arranged times, corporations could hold transatlantic meetings transmitted by satellite. At $5,000 an hour, the exciting technological advance came at a cost too steep for customers still unfamiliar with how computers, cell phones, and fax machines would revolutionize business practices. The experiment was short-lived.

Starting in 1981 InterContinental was bought and sold by a succession of international companies. But The Barclay worked to maintain its style and reputation as a Midtown getaway for discerning travelers through each corporate transition. As of 2001 the hotel once again included the name "Barclay" into its official title. The corner of 48th and Lexington Avenue reclaimed a piece of its history.

Looking Forward

The fourteen-story, beige, brick and limestone, neo-Federal Barclay Hotel stands in stately defiance to the modern skyscrapers towering above it.

At the time of this writing, Midtown East is poised to go through yet another reversal. The mayor wants to rezone the area around Grand Central Terminal to increase development and density in order to expand, once again, the corporate presence in the neighborhood.

The changes would allow developers to compile parcels of land and demolish the existing properties to make way for bigger, taller, more profitable buildings. The opening of the long-awaited Second Avenue subway line within a few years is also expected to increase new opportunities along the Midtown corridor.

Preservationists trying to maintain some of the district's historic character have identified The Barclay as one of its older, most vulnerable buildings. Alex Herrera, with the New York Landmarks Conservancy, believes that, "these structures are not obsolete, low-ceilinged disposable construction, but rather represent some of the best architecture in the area, designed by distinguished architects." Since The Barclay does not currently have landmark status like its neighbor, The Waldorf-Astoria, its future existence remains uncertain.

New York City's preservation movement has strong connections to the neighborhood. When Penn Central took control of Grand Central Terminal, it proposed demolishing or reconfiguring the terminal and replacing it with an office building in the late 1960s. The process went so far as to solicit designs for skyscrapers from famed modern architects I. M. Pei and Marcel Breuer. An active grassroots campaign—including involvement by former First Lady Jacqueline Kennedy Onassis who became the public face of the Committee to Save Grand Central Station—and New York City's relatively new Landmarks Preservation Commission rescued the majestic structure.

The Commission had in part been created as a response to the cultural disaster that occurred with the demolition of the spectacular Pennsylvania Station across town on West 34th Street. Concerned New Yorkers mobilized to avoid another similar loss. In 1967 Grand Central Terminal received its landmark status, which offers a building greater protection from destruction or major architectural changes. The development plans crumbled instead of the station.

Most of The Barclay's sister hotels and comparably classic apartment houses on Park Avenue have already been razed for taller, sleeker, and more profitable office towers. The Biltmore was dismantled and rebuilt as the Bank of America building in 1984. Its fabled clock now sits watch over the security guards' desk in the lobby. The Commodore's original structure was stripped down to its steel frame, given a new glass façade, and re-opened as The Grand Hyatt in 1980 as one of the Trump Organization's first major projects. The Roosevelt has been bought and sold and threatened with demolition several times but, for now, still operates as a hotel. The Park Lane Hotel, another property once owned by The New York State Realty and Terminal Company located to the west of The Barclay on 48th Street, was replaced with a 42-story skyscraper in 1967. Even the public street between The Barclay and The Park Lane, one of the shortest in 1920s Manhattan, was destroyed along with hotel.

The Barclay is one of the few remaining structures developed as part of the Terminal City project. As it is now being considered in the same league as iconic monuments like Grand Central and

Pennsylvania Stations, preservationists recognize that the hotel has special value to the city. Given The Barclay's numerous connections to the Vanderbilt family, world-renowned architects and designers, Prohibition, Broadway, classic American literature, Miss America, the Civil Rights Movement, New York institutions likes the Metropolitan Museum of Art and the Metropolitan Opera, and scores of legendary cultural, political, and diplomatic figures, it is indisputable that the hotel embodies a unique part of New York City's history.

In 1965 the architecture critic Ada Louise Huxtable wrote, "What preservation is really all about is the retention and active relationship of the buildings of the past to the community's functioning present." Whether or not The Barclay continues its physical relationship with its Midtown neighborhood, its legacy will remain intact.

Selected Bibliography

General References

Personal interviews with past and present staff conducted by authors between February and December 2012.

Landmarks Preservation Commission, *General Electric Building* (LP-1412), July 9, 1985, Designation List 181.

The New York Central Railroad Company, *Report of the Board of Directors to the Stockholders,* 1931- 1938.

Books

Ballon, Hilary and Kenneth T. Jackson, ed. *Robert Moses and the Modern City: The Transformation of New York.* New York: W. W. Norton & Company, 2008.

Caro, Robert A. *The Power Broker: Robert Moses and the Fall of New York.* New York: Vintage Books, 1975.

Drowne, Kathleen Morgan and Patrick Huber. *The 1920s.* Connecticut: Greenwood Publishing Group, 2004.

Gelb, Arthur and Barbara. *O'Neill: Life with Monte Cristo.* New York: Applause Theater Books, 2002.

Hotchner, A. E. *Papa Hemingway: A Personal Memoir.* Boston: Da Capo Press, 2005.

Jackson, Kenneth T. and Fred Kameny, ed. *Almanac of New York City.* New York: Columbia University Press, 2008.

Mesta, Perle Skirvin. *Perle: My Story*. New York: McGraw-Hill, 1960.

Monkkonen, Eric H. *Murder in New York City*. Berkeley: University of California Press, 2001.

Nevins, Deborah, ed. *Grand Central Terminal: City Within the City*. New York: The Municipal Art Society of New York, 1982.

Ponselle, Rosa and James A. Drake. *Ponselle: A Singer's Life*. New York: Doubleday, 1982.

Renehan, Edward J., Jr. Commodore: *The Life of Cornelius Vanderbilt*. New York: Basic Books, 2007.

Reynolds, Michael. *Hemingway: The Final Years*. New York: W. W. Norton & Company, 2000.

Rose, Kenneth D. *American Women and the Repeal of Prohibition*. New York: New York University Press, 1996.

Sandoval-Strausz, A. K. Hotel: *An American History*. Connecticut: Yale University Press, 2008.

Vanderbilt, Arthur T. II. *Fortune's Children: The Fall of the House of Vanderbilt*. New York: William Morrow, 1989.

Vreeland, Diana. *D.V.* Boston: Da Capo Press, 2003.

Articles

"The Last El Train," *New York Daily News*, March 25, 2009.

"Widow From Oklahoma," *Time*, March 14, 1949.

Beale, Betty. "Treasury Secretary Newest Idol of Mrs. Perle Mesta," *The Spokesman Review,* April 1, 1972.

Davidson, Alex. "Miss America's Makeover," *Forbes*, January 29, 2007.

King, Martin Luther, Jr. "My Talk with Ben Bella," *The New York Amsterdam News,* October 27, 1962.

Selected Bibliography

Plimpton, George. "Great Days Under Sail," *Sports Illustrated*, October 15, 1956.

Rogers, Cleveland. "Robert Moses," *The Atlantic Magazine*, February 1939.

Wilson, Earl. "Eugene O'Neill Let Us in on Why *The Iceman Cometh*." *New York Post*, August 2, 1946.

New York Times:

"Bedlam on Radio Row," May 25, 1930.

"Ben Bella Links Two 'Injustices,'" October 14, 1962.

"Big Apartments for Sutton Place," October 22, 1921.

"East Side Chemists Hark Back to 1752," February 12, 1952.

"Eugene O'Neill Dies of Pneumonia; Playwright, 65, Won Nobel Prize," November 28, 1953.

"Get a Home De Luxe in Biltmore Hotel," September 29, 1912.

"Lexington Avenue Changing Rapidly," May 6, 1928.

"Roosevelt Hotel to Open Sept. 22," September 14, 1924.

"Soda Fountain Gushes Champagne, Too, As Drug Store Celebrates Its 200th Year," March 27, 1952.

Bernstein, Fred A. "Makeover at Grand Hyatt Sheds the Trump Glitter," January 11, 2011.

Chan, Sewell. "Is Overdevelopment Still a Threat?," October 22, 2008.

Dunlap, David W. "A Boy's View of New York, 50 Years Ago," February 24, 2012.

—. "It's Possible To Meet Again Under The Biltmore Clock," May 16, 1984.

Feretti, Fred. "Occupancy in Hotels Running at 90%," November 14, 1978.

Gray, Christopher. "Grand Central; Covering Its Tracks Paid Off Handsomely," August 22, 2010.

—. "The Former Vanderbilt Hotel, 34th Street and Park Avenue; It Was a Showcase for Terra Cotta. Much Remains," March 09, 2003.

Hammer, Alexander R. "Pennsy Sets Sale of Barclay Hotel," August 10, 1972.

Horsley, Carter B. "From Brick to Glass in Grand Central Area," March 11, 1979.

—. "Three Prominent Midtown Hotels Sold; Two May be Turned Into Apartments," July 29, 1978.

Kaiser, Charles. "Last Guest Checks Out of the Commodore Hotel," May 19, 1976.

Kramer, Hilton. "The Culture Scene in 1976: Key People and Creations," December 26, 1976.

Lyons, Richard D. "Manhattan Hotels Break the $200 Barrier," November 30, 1986.

McDowell, Edwin. "British Brewer Will Buy Big Hotel Chain," February 21, 1998.

Owens, Emily G. "The (Not So) Roaring '20s," October 1, 2011.

Sterne, Michael. "A Sales Pitch for New York," December 11, 1977.

Van Gelder, Robert. "Ernest Hemingway Talks of Work and War," August 11, 1940.

Whitman, Alden. "Reigned for 30 Years—Perle Mesta, Hostess to the Politically Famous, Is Dead," March 17, 1975.

www.ingramcontent.com/pod-product-compliance
Lightning Source LLC
Chambersburg PA
CBHW071626170426
43195CB00038B/2142